WILLI ELSENER
MENUS & MUSIC FOR CHRISTMAS

WILLI ELSENER

MENUS & MUSIC FOR CHRISTMAS

TRADITIONAL CHRISTMAS CAROLS
CLASSIC CHRISTMAS RECIPES

MACMILLAN • USA

With grateful thanks to my wife, Jayne Elsener
The Dorchester Management
Colin Webb, Publisher
Caroline Davidson, Literary Agent
Sylvia Baumann, Jamie Walker, Brenda Martin, Elish Browning
and all other helping hands

MACMILLAN
A Simon & Schuster Macmillan Company
1633 Broadway
New York, NY 10019-6785

Library of Congress Cataloging-in-Publication Data
Elsener, Willi
  Menus and music for Christmas/Willi Elsener
  p. cm.
  Includes index.
  ISBN 0-02-861398-8 (alk. paper)
  1. Christmas cookery. 2. Menus. 3. Christmas. 4. Christmas music. I. Title.
TX739.2.C45E44 1996
641.5 68--dc20   96-31121
                                                                            CIP

ISBN: 0-02-861398-8

Printed in China
CD manufactured in Germany

10 9 8 7 6 5 4 3 2 1

FRONTISPIECE: DORCHESTER CHRISTMAS PUDDING

CONTENTS

INTRODUCTION

Christmas is a time of celebration the world over. While traditions may vary, there is an international spirit of festivity – a feeling of something magical in the air.

In researching for this book, I have learned how little I knew about the origins of Christmas, let alone the customs and foods that accompany celebrations around the world. Talking to friends and colleagues has been enlightening: so often tradition varies not only from country to country, but also from region to region, and even within families. In spite of this, one common theme has evolved, which is that food is the basis around which all celebrations revolve.

Our celebrations centre on Christmas Day, the date of Jesus Christ's birth – or is it? This fact is far from certain! Rather it appears to be the result of a calculated decision by Pope Julius I in the fourth century. By placing 'Christmas' in the middle of the ancient pagan midwinter festivities, he hoped to absorb and convert the masses. To a certain extent he succeeded but many old pagan customs linger on, varying from country to country and resulting in the diverse traditions that exist across the world today.

While I could not hope to cover all of these, I have endeavoured to capture some of them. This book is presented in twelve chapters, each consisting of a menu containing at least one dish inspired by a particular country and complemented by others created from my imagination. Some dishes are based on actual recipes handed down across the generations, while others are specially created for the festive season in general and this book in particular.

In introducing each menu, I have made reference to a particular country and I have tried to share with you some of the interesting information I have gathered about its customs and, in particular, a speciality dish. Each recipe, too, has a brief introduction which refers perhaps to origin, taste or technique. While some recipes are new and creative, these have not been included at the expense of tradition. The traditions of Christmas are brought to life in no small way by the magical sounds of its seasonal music. I can still remember standing as a small boy, wide-eyed on a snowy Christmas Eve, listening to the joyous sound of carols being sung outside the hotel.

As families the world over trim the tree, the sound of carols fills the air, capturing the meaning of Christmas. While it may be the season of goodwill, of joy and fun, it is also a time of hard work for the cook in the family. But what nicer way to cook than to do so accompanied by these songs! I hope that together, this book and its accompanying CD will relieve some of the pressure and inspire you to enliven old favourites and adventure with new creations.

If you enjoy the excitement of experimenting, sampling alternative recipes and dabbling with different ingredients, then this collection is for you. While I cannot guarantee to take the stress out of Christmas cooking, you can rest assured that each recipe is tried and tested twice over… and is most definitely delicious! You, your family and friends will certainly delight in the results as you feast surrounded by twinkling lights and the magical sounds of Christmas.

WILLI ELSENER 1996

*T*his is, in truth, not a menu at all, but rather an opportunity to share with you some favourite recipes to prepare on 'Stir-up Sunday', which is the last Sunday before Advent. Traditionally, it's our last chance to make puddings and cakes so that they're ready in time for Christmas Day. I hope you'll enjoy these recipes, which include the famous Dorchester Christmas Pudding and an old family favourite. The Lazy Christmas Loaf is for those of you who are short on time! From my own experience, it's fun to let the family join in. Remember that everyone should have a stir of the pudding and make a wish. The rather quaint name of Stir-up Sunday comes not from this culinary activity, however, but rather from the Collect in the service for that day: 'Stir up we beseech thee, O Lord, the wills of thy faithful people, that they plenteously bringing forth the fruits of good works, may of thee be plenteously rewarded.'

GRANNY'S FRUIT CAKE

*T*his is simply one of the best fruit cakes I have ever eaten. It is densely packed with fruit, very moist and keeps for ages. At home it never lasts long enough even to get iced, but it can obviously have the traditional treatment with almond and royal icings. I prefer to decorate with a glazed fruit and nut topping, which is quick and easy.

MAKES 1 CAKE

2²/₃ cups/450 g/1 lb mixed dried fruit
1²/₃ cups/225 g/8 oz mixed glacé fruit, chopped
½ cup/75 g/3 oz glacé cherries, quartered
1½ cups/275 g/10 oz sugar
1 cup/225 g/8 oz butter
1¼ cups/300 ml/10 fl oz water
3½ cups/350 g/12 oz plain flour
1 pinch salt
1 tsp mixed spice (or ½ tsp ground cinnamon, ½ tsp nutmeg)
½ tsp ground cinnamon
1½ tsp bicarbonate of soda (baking soda)
1 cup/100 g/4 oz flaked almonds
2 eggs, beaten
1 tsp almond essence
2 tbsp brandy

FOR THE ROYAL ICING (OPTIONAL):
1 egg white
1½ cups/275 g/10 oz icing (confectioner's) sugar

FOR THE TOPPING:
2 cups/350g/12 oz mixed glacé fruit
12 walnut halves
1 cup/350 g/12 oz apricot jam
2 tbsp brandy

To prepare the tin, line the base and sides of an 8 inch/20 cm square tin, or a 9 inch/23 cm round tin about 3 inches/7.5 cm deep, with a single layer of greased silicone paper. Wrap 12 layers of newspaper, cut to size, around the tin and secure with sellotape and string. This will prevent the cake from drying out during the cooking process.

To make the cake, place the mixed fruit, glacé fruit, cherries, sugar, butter and water together in a large pan. Slowly bring to the boil, then simmer gently for 10 minutes. Allow to cool.

Sift together the flour, salt, cinnamon, spice and bicarbonate of soda (baking soda). Add this, together with the almonds, to the cold fruit mixture.

Lightly whisk together the eggs, almond essence and brandy, and add to the cake mixture. Mix together thoroughly using a wooden spoon.

Spoon into the prepared tin. Place 12 layers of newspaper on the oven shelf and sit the cake tin on top of this. Bake in the preheated oven, at 325°F/170°C/gas mark 3 for 2½ hours. After 1 hour, check the cake and if it is browning too quickly, cover with a piece of foil.

When the cake is cooked, remove from the oven and cover with a clean dry tea towel. Allow to cool thoroughly before turning out. When cold, it can be wrapped in foil until ready to decorate. It will mature well for up to 3 months.

If you wish to ice the cake, whisk the egg white until frothy, gradually stir in the sieved icing (confectioner's) sugar and mix thoroughly until the icing forms stiff peaks. It needs to be really firm to pipe with. If necessary, add a little more icing (confectioner's) sugar.

Turn the cake upside-down. Ensure that it is flat and use the base of the cake as the top surface. Put the jam and brandy together in a pan, and heat until boiling. Push through a sieve. Using a brush, generously coat the top of the cake with the glaze.

Either arrange the fruits and nuts over the top or, alternatively, if you are using Royal icing as in the picture, first pipe a border of icing along the top edge and then place the fruits in the middle. Brush the fruits and nuts generously again with the apricot glaze. Cool and store for up to 1 month. Before serving, decorate with a ribbon.

LAZY CHRISTMAS LOAF

This has got to be one of the quickest, easiest Christmas cakes ever. In fact, it's delicious all year through! Serve it simply as it is or decorate with a glazed fruit and nut topping, as suggested for Granny's Fruit Cake on page 8.

MAKES 1 LOAF

2⅔ cups/450 g/1 lb mixed dried fruit
⅓ cup/50g/2 oz glacé cherries, quartered
1 cup/175 g/6 oz dark brown sugar
1¼ cups/300 ml/10 fl oz cold strong tea
½ cup/50 g/2 oz flaked almonds
1 cup/150 g/5 oz self-raising flour
2 eggs, slightly beaten
icing (confectioner's) sugar

To prepare the tin, line and grease the base and sides of a 2 lb/900 g loaf tin: 12 in/30 cm x 3 in/8 cm x 2½ in/6 cm.

To make the loaf, mix together the fruit, cherries, sugar and cold tea. Cover with clingfilm and leave to soak overnight.

Next day, add the almonds, flour and lightly beaten eggs. Mix well together and pour into the prepared tin. Bake in a preheated oven at 300°F/150°C/gas mark 2 for 2½ hours until cooked. Check the loaf after 1 hour and if it is browning too quickly cover with a sheet of foil.

When the cake is cooked, remove from the oven and allow to cool slightly before removing from the tin. Then allow the loaf to cool completely on a wire rack. Dust with sifted icing (confectioner's) sugar before serving. Serve within 1 week or freeze for up to 3 months.

RIGHT: GRANNY'S FRUIT CAKE

STOLLEN

This is a delicious rich fruit bread, originating in Dresden, Germany. Stollen is also eaten in Austria and my native Switzerland over the festive season. It takes a while to rise because of the large quantity of fruit, but it is well worth the wait. My family enjoy it for breakfast, thinly sliced with butter.

MAKES 1 LOAF

⅓ cup/40g/1½ oz currants
⅓ cup/40g/1½ oz sultanas (sultana raisins)
⅓ cup/40g/1½ oz glacé cherries, quartered
⅓ cup/40g/1½ oz mixed (citrus) peel, chopped
¼ cup/50 ml/2 fl oz rum

⅔ cup/150 ml/5 fl oz milk
6 tbsp/75 g/3 oz caster (granulated) sugar
1 heaped tbsp dried active baking yeast
⅓ cup/150 g/5 oz unsalted butter
2½ cups/350 g/12 oz strong white bread flour
1 large egg, lightly beaten
½ tsp salt

¼ cup/25 g/1 oz flaked almonds
rind of ½ lemon, grated

FOR THE GLAZE:
1 tbsp/25 g/1 oz butter, melted
2 tbsp caster (granulated) sugar
½ tsp ground cinnamon
icing (confectioner's) sugar to dredge

Place the currants, sultanas, cherries and mixed peel in a small pan. Pour over the rum. Slowly bring to the boil, boil for 1 minute, then remove from the heat and allow to cool.

Meanwhile, heat half the milk until just tepid. Pour it into a bowl, add 1 tsp of the sugar and sprinkle over the yeast. Whisk well, then cover with clingfilm and leave in a warm, draught-free place for about 10–15 minutes until frothy.

In another pan, bring the remaining milk to the boil. Remove from the heat and add the remaining sugar and the butter. Leave to one side, stirring occasionally, until the sugar has dissolved and the butter melted. When the mixture is tepid and the yeast mixture frothy, combine the two and whisk together.

Now sift the flour and salt into a large bowl. Make a well in the centre and pour in the milk mixture and the egg. Work the mixture together well with your hands to form a dough.

Add the flaked almonds and lemon rind to the soaked fruit, and add this to the dough. Work the mixture together with your hands until it leaves the bowl cleanly. Turn out on to a floured board and knead for 5 minutes until smooth and elastic.

Place the dough in a lightly greased bowl, cover with a damp cloth and leave in a warm draught-free place for about 1½ hours until doubled in size. Turn the dough on to a lightly floured board. Knock it back and knead until smooth, then roll it with your hands into a rectangle about 12 inches/30 cm by 6 inches/15 cm. Fold in half lengthwise. Carefully place the loaf on a lined and greased baking sheet, allowing room for expansion. Leave it in a warm place for about 30–40 minutes, until doubled in size.

Bake in a preheated oven at 350°F/180°C/gas mark 4 for 10 minutes. Then reduce the heat to 300°F/150°C/gas mark 2, and bake for a further 30–40 minutes until cooked.

Just before removing it from the oven, melt the butter for the glaze and mix together the sugar and cinnamon. Remove the loaf from the oven and immediately brush with the melted butter and sprinkle with the sugar and cinnamon. Allow to cool. Just before serving, dust generously with icing (confectioner's) sugar.

RIGHT: STOLLEN

NORWEGIAN PLAIT

A good alternative to Stollen, this plaited bread is delicious sliced and generously spread with butter. Serve with a steaming mug of tea or coffee.

MAKES 1 LOAF

1 tsp caster (granulated) sugar	½ tsp salt
1¼ cups/300 ml/10 fl oz lukewarm milk	⅓ cup/150 g/5 oz mixed dried fruit
1 tbsp dried, active baking yeast	¾ cup/25 g/1 oz mixed (citrus) peel, chopped
3 cups/450 g/1 lb strong white bread flour	⅓ cup/50 g/2 oz nibbed almonds
¼ cup/50 g/2 oz unsalted butter, cubed (at room temperature)	beaten egg to brush the plait a little sugar to sprinkle over

Dissolve the sugar in half the milk. Sprinkle the dried yeast over this and whisk well. Cover with clingfilm. Allow the mixture to stand in a warm draught-free place for 10–15 minutes until frothy.

Meanwhile, sift together the flour and salt, and rub in the butter. Add the mixed dried fruit, chopped peel and half of the almonds. When the yeast mixture is ready, whisk it gently and pour over the dry ingredients. Add the remaining tepid milk and mix to a soft dough. Cover with a damp cloth and leave to rise in a warm draught-free place for 1 hour.

Knead the mixture gently and divide into 3 equal pieces. Using your hands, gently roll each piece into a long sausage shape of equal lengths, about 16 inches/40 cm long. Plait together loosely, turning the ends under to seal. Place on a lined and greased baking tray and leave to rise again for 30 minutes.

Bake in a preheated oven at 375°F/190°C/gas mark 5 for 15 minutes. Remove and brush with a little beaten egg, then sprinkle over a little sugar and the remaining nuts. Bake for a further 10 minutes. Remove and place on a wire rack. Allow to cool and serve.

CHRISTMAS MINCEMEAT

Traditionally, mincemeat contained minced beef, giving it a much milder flavour then we are used to today. This recipe gives a rich luxurious mincemeat, perfect for all manner of desserts and, of course, mince pies (see page 56).

MAKES ABOUT ENOUGH FOR 50 MINCE PIES/1¾ LB/800 G

1 cup/100 g/4 oz pared and sliced cooking apple
⅔ cup/100 g/4 oz raisins
⅔ cup/100 g/4 oz currants
⅔ cup/100 g/4 oz sultanas (sultana raisins)
¼ cup/25 g/1 oz glacé ginger, finely chopped
⅓ cup/50 g/2 oz glacé cherries, finely chopped
1½ cups/50 g/2 oz mixed (citrus) peel, finely chopped
¼ cup/25 g/1 oz blanched slivered almonds
¼ cup/100 g/4 oz shredded suet (animal fat)
¾ cup/150 g/5 oz soft brown sugar
grated rind and juice of 2 lemons
¼ tsp ground cinnamon
¼ tsp ground nutmeg
⅛ tsp ground cloves
4 tbsp/50 ml/2 fl oz brandy

Peel, core and chop the apples very finely. Place in a large bowl and add all the other ingredients. Mix well. Cover the bowl with a clean cloth and leave the mixture to marinate in a cool place for 48 hours. Stir occasionally.

The mincemeat may be used now, or packed into clean dry jars and sealed.

DORCHESTER CHRISTMAS PUDDING

This is the ultimate Christmas pudding: light, yet deliciously fruity. The recipe makes 1 large pudding – enough for about 10 portions. If you prefer, make two smaller puddings but allow the same cooking time. Remember that a Christmas pudding should be made at least one month in advance in order to allow time for the flavours to develop and mature.

SERVES 10

1½ cups/100 g/4 oz currants
1½ cups/100 g/4 oz sultanas (sultana raisins)
1½ cups/100 g/4 oz raisins
1½ cups/100 g/4 oz mixed (citrus) peel
⅛ cup/15 g/½ oz crystallized ginger, chopped
½ cup/40 g/1½ oz grated apple (preferably Cox's Orange Pippin)
⅛ cup/15 g/½ oz prunes, (roughly chopped)
½ orange (zest and juice)
½ lemon (zest and juice)
1½ tbsp/65 g/2½ oz soft brown sugar
4 tbsp Guinness (or any stout beer)
4 tbsp ale
2 tbsp brandy

2 tbsp sweet sherry
2 eggs
2 tbsp milk
½ cup/65 g/2½ oz plain flour
3 tbsp mixed spice (or 2 tsp each of ground cinnamon, ground ginger and ground cloves)
1 tsp salt
⅛ cup/15 g/½ oz ground almonds
1½ cups/75 g/3 oz fresh breadcrumbs
½ cup/100 g/4 oz shredded suet (animal fat)

TO FINISH (OPTIONAL):
caster (granulated) sugar
brandy

Mix all the fruit together with the sugar in a large bowl, then add all the alcohol. Marinate the mixture in the refrigerator for at least 24 hours.

Beat together the eggs and milk, then add to the fruit mixture. Add the remaining ingredients and mix together with a spoon until thoroughly combined. Cover and refrigerate. Leave to mature for 5–7 days. Spoon into a 1¾ pint/1 litre greased pudding basin. Cover securely with clingfilm, then tin foil, then the lid. If the basin doesn't have a lid, cover with a pudding cloth and tie securely.

Steam in a saucepan for about 4–5 hours. To do this, put a ring or upturned plate into the bottom of a large saucepan. Put the pudding basin on the centre of the ring or plate. Add enough water to fill the pan to just beneath the bottom rim of the pudding basin. Bring the water to the boil, cover the saucepan and simmer. Replenish the water as necessary, making sure that the pan does not boil dry.

After steaming, allow it to cool and then cover with fresh greaseproof paper and store in a cool dry place to allow it to mature.

Before serving, renew the greaseproof paper and steam in the same way as described above for about 3 hours.

Turn out on to a hot dish, sprinkle with sugar and pour some warm brandy over it. Flame carefully and serve.

*F*or this menu, I have drawn inspiration from American Thanksgiving Day. In the USA, with its diverse cultural background, Thanksgiving is the traditional celebration of the year rather than Christmas. It's a time when family and friends are reunited to give thanks and celebrate. The custom dates back to 1621, when the Pilgrims set aside a day for thanksgiving after their first harvest. Now it's observed throughout the USA on the fourth Thursday each November. While acknowledging this tradition with a turkey, I have introduced an unusual pecan nut and pine kernel stuffing. Alternatively, try the duck breast with sultanas and cranberries. As a starter, I propose succulent scallops and mussels with a coriander sauce flavoured with pink peppercorns which give a little sharpness. Dessert is my interpretation of the all-American apple pie!

Scallops and Mussels in Pink Peppercorn and Coriander (Cilantro) Sauce

*T*he succulent fresh scallops enhanced by the passion fruit and the sharpness of the pink peppercorns are what makes this dish special.

Serves 4

6 tbsp vegetable oil
12 medium mussels, cleaned and unopened
1 shallot, finely chopped
7 tbsp/100 ml/3½ fl oz dry white wine
16 large scallops, roe removed

For the Sauce:
stock from above
pulp of 1 passion fruit
1¼ cups/300 ml/10 fl oz fish stock
1 cup/250 ml/8 fl oz double (heavy) cream
1 tbsp diced carrot
1 tbsp diced leek
salt and freshly ground pepper
1 tsp chopped coriander (cilantro) leaves
1 tsp pink peppercorns in brine, strained
fresh dill and chervil to garnish

Heat 2 tbsp of vegetable oil in a saucepan and add the mussels. Stir, add the chopped shallots and sweat for 1 minute. Add the white wine, bring to the boil and cover. Simmer for 4 minutes until the mussels open, discarding any that do not open. Remove the mussels with a perforated spoon and set aside.

To make the sauce, boil the mussel stock rapidly until reduced by half. Add the fish stock and the passion fruit pulp, then boil rapidly until reduced by half again. Add the cream and strain through a fine sieve into another saucepan. Add the diced carrot and leek, and bring rapidly to the boil. Then simmer over medium heat, stirring frequently, until a creamy consistency is obtained. Set aside.

Pat the scallops dry on a paper towel, and season with salt and pepper. Heat the remaining 4 tbsp of vegetable oil in a non-stick pan, and brown the scallops on both sides. Cook over medium heat until cooked by still moist inside, then remove from the pan.

Arrange 4 scallops in a circle on each plate, then place 3 mussels in the centre of the circle. Bring the sauce to the boil and add the chopped coriander (cilantro) and pink peppercorns. Pour over the scallops and garnish with dill and chervil.

ROAST TURKEY WITH PECAN NUT AND PINE KERNEL STUFFING

A fresh bird is best, but if you opt for a frozen turkey, ensure that it is completely thawed before stuffing and cooking. I picked up this method of roasting turkey in a muslin cloth in America. It results in a lovely, golden-brown, moist bird.

SERVES 8

10–12 lb/4.5–5.5 kg oven-ready turkey
with giblets
1 onion, peeled
1 cup/225 g/8 oz butter, softened
1 tsp fresh chopped sage
salt and paprika to taste

FOR THE PECAN NUT AND PINE KERNEL
STUFFING:
2 tbsp/30 ml vegetable oil
1 onion, chopped
1¼ cups/150 g/5 oz pecan nuts, coarsely
chopped
1¼ cups/150 g/5 oz pine nuts, coarsely
chopped
9 oz/250 g pork sausagemeat

2 tsp chopped sage
1 tsp finely chopped parsley
4 tsp breadcrumbs
salt and freshly ground pepper

FOR THE GRAVY:
2½ cups/600 ml/1 pint chicken stock
1 tbsp cornflour (cornstarch) or
arrowroot

Remove the giblets from the turkey and keep refrigerated until required. Wash the turkey well and dry with kitchen paper both inside and out.

To prepare the stuffing, heat the vegetable oil in a saucepan, add the onion and sweat until translucent but not coloured. Add the pecan nuts and pine kernels, and allow to cool. Mix in the sausagemeat, sage, parsley, breadcrumbs, salt and pepper.

Loosely fill the neck cavity with the stuffing, pushing it gently up beneath the skin towards the breast. Pull the skin flap down under the bird and secure with a skewer. Weigh the dressed bird and calculate the cooking time. A 12–14 lb/5.5–6.5 kg bird (including stuffing) will need 4–4¾ hours.

Salt the body cavity and rub it with the sage. Cut the onion in 4 lengthways and place in the cavity. Now rub the bird all over with the butter, and sprinkle generously with salt and paprika. Place breast side up in the roasting tray and cover completely with a double layer of muslin. Place in the preheated oven at

425°F/220°C/gas mark 7. After 30 minutes, baste the turkey with the butter and reduce the temperature to 325°F/170°C/gas mark 3. Return the turkey to the oven for a further 3½–4¼ hours, according to size. Baste at 30-minute intervals.

To check that the turkey is cooked, pierce the thigh with a skewer. when it is cooked, the juices will run clear with no trace of pink. Remove the muslin, place the turkey on a warm platter and cover with foil. Allow to rest in a warm place for 30–45 minutes before carving.

Meanwhile, make the gravy. Place the giblets in the roasting tray and return to the oven. Increase the heat to 425°F/220°C/gas mark 7, and cook for 10–15 minutes, turning once, until brown all over. Remove from the oven and pour off excess fat. Place the tray on top of the hob over medium heat. Pour over the chicken stock and allow to simmer for 10 minutes. Dissolve the cornflour (cornstarch) or arrowroot in a little cold water and whisk it in. Allow to simmer for a few minutes to thicken. Strain and adjust seasoning. Keep warm until required.

LEFT: SCALLOPS AND MUSSELS IN PINK PEPPERCORN
AND CORIANDER (CILANTRO) SAUCE

CRANBERRY SAUCE

The sharp flavour of this sauce complements the turkey. It is a traditional accompaniment to the Thanksgiving meal, and has also been adopted in the UK for the Christmas table since World War Two. The sauce can be made up a week in advance and kept covered in the refrigerator.

SERVES 8

2 cups/225 g/8 oz fresh cranberries
½ cup/100 g/4 oz demerara (granulated) sugar
½ tsp freshly grated root ginger
1 cinnamon stick about 1 inch/2.5 cm long
3 cloves
¼ tsp ground allspice
⅓ cup/75 ml/3 fl oz water
⅓ cup/75 ml/3 fl oz cider vinegar
2 tbsp port

Wash the cranberries and put them in a saucepan. Add the sugar, ginger, cinnamon, cloves and allspice. Pour over the vinegar and place over gentle heat, stirring occasionally, until all the sugar has dissolved. Then bring to the boil over moderate heat and simmer, uncovered, until the cranberries are soft and beginning to burst. Remove from the heat, add the port, and allow to cool. Remove the cinnamon stick. Turn into a serving dish and cover with clingfilm until required.

RIGHT: ROAST TURKEY WITH PECAN NUT AND PINE KERNEL STUFFING

DUCK BREAST WITH SULTANAS AND CRANBERRIES

For a smaller gathering, rather than cook a whole turkey, try these duck breasts served in a fruity cranberry sauce. Cook them only until lightly pink for the best result.

SERVES 4

4 medium duck breasts
salt and freshly ground pepper
2 tbsp vegetable oil

FOR THE SAUCE:
2 tbsp cranberries
½ small shallot, finely chopped
5 cardamom pods, crushed
1 tsp butter
1 cup/200 ml/7 fl oz red wine
1 cup/200 ml/7 fl oz port
1 cup/200 ml/7 fl oz chicken stock
1 tsp cornflour (cornstarch)
2 tsp water
1 tbsp sultanas (sultana raisins), soaked in water for 10 minutes and drained
salt and freshly ground white pepper

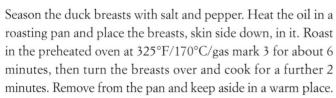

Season the duck breasts with salt and pepper. Heat the oil in a roasting pan and place the breasts, skin side down, in it. Roast in the preheated oven at 325°F/170°C/gas mark 3 for about 6 minutes, then turn the breasts over and cook for a further 2 minutes. Remove from the pan and keep aside in a warm place.

To make the sauce, cook the cranberries in boiling water for 30 seconds. Refresh in cold water. Drain and set aside.

In a saucepan, sweat the shallots and cardamom pods in butter until the shallots are translucent but not coloured. Add the red wine, boil rapidly until half the quantity remains. Add the port and stock, and boil rapidly again until reduced by half. Dissolve the cornflour (cornstarch) in cold water, add to the sauce and cook for 2 minutes. Pass the mixture through a sieve into a saucepan. Add the sultanas and cranberries and bring to the boil. Season with salt and white pepper.

Arrange the duck breasts on plates and pour 1–2 spoons of the cranberry and sultana sauce on top. Serve the remaining sauce separately.

SWEET POTATO AND MUSHROOM CAKES

This is a tasty alternative to the roast sweet potatoes traditionally served with the Thanksgiving meal. They're easy to make, but it's crucial that you don't grate the potatoes until just before cooking or they'll turn brown.

SERVES 4

2 tbsp/25 g/1 oz butter
2 cups/100 g/4 oz button mushrooms, finely chopped
½ tbsp finely chopped parsley
½ tbsp finely chopped chives
4 tbsp vegetable oil
3 tbsp medium potatoes
5 oz/150 g sweet potatoes
2 tsp cornflour (cornstarch)
salt and freshly ground pepper

Heat the butter in a non-stick pan. Add the chopped mushrooms and fry gently for 1 minute. Remove the mushrooms from the pan and place in a fine sieve. Press gently to drain off as much liquid as possible. Allow to cool, then place the mushrooms in a large bowl. Add the parsley and chives and set aside.

Shortly before cooking, grate the potatoes and sweet potatoes with a fine hand grater and mix together well. Take the grated mixture between your hands and press out any excess liquid. Then mix with the mushrooms and herbs. Sprinkle the cornflour (cornstarch) on it and mix thoroughly. Divide the mixture into 8 equal portions and start cooking these immediately.

Heat some oil in a non-stick pan. Take one portion and remove any remaining excess liquid with your hand. Form the potato into a small round cake shape approximately 5 mm/½ inch thick. Fry in the pan on both sides until cooked and golden brown. Season with salt and pepper. Remove from the pan and place on kitchen paper. Keep warm until required.

SEARED CAULIFLOWER AND SWEET PEPPERS

This is a colourful dish which perfectly complements the richness of the rest of the meal. It's equally good made with broccoli, or even a mixture of both.

SERVES 4

1 medium cauliflower, florets only
4 tbsp olive oil
1 medium onion, cut into ½ inch/1 cm cubes
1 yellow pepper (bell pepper), deseeded and cut into
½ inch/1 cm cubes
1 red pepper (bell pepper), deseeded and cut into
½ inch/1 cm cubes
salt and freshly ground pepper

Boil the cauliflower florets in lightly salted water until cooked but still crisp. Refresh under cold water, drain and set aside.

Heat half the oil in a non-stick pan and add the onion and pepper. Fry, covered, over medium heat until golden brown and cooked. Season, remove from the pan and set aside.

Clean the pan with kitchen towel and add the remaining oil. Add the cauliflower florets, heat, browning on all sides, and season. Mix in the peppers and stir. Place in a serving dish and serve hot.

APPLE AND CREAM CHEESE PIE

This is a glorious apple concoction. Tart apple slices in a creamy filling, encased in a light pastry case – what better way to end a Thanksgiving meal?

SERVES 6–8

FOR THE PASTRY:
melted butter for greasing, flour for dusting
14 oz/400 g shortcrust pastry (pastry crust)

FOR THE FILLING:
½ cup/90 g/3½ oz sugar
2 tbsp plain flour
3 eggs
2 egg yolks
1 cup/200 g/7 oz mascarpone cheese
2 tsp ground cinnamon

¼ tsp ground nutmeg
1 tsp finely grated lemon zest
2 tbsp/25 g/1 oz butter for cooking the apples
6 cups/600 g/1 lb 5 oz Granny Smith apples, peeled,
cored and sliced
3 tbsp smooth apricot jam
⅔ cup/50 g/2 oz toasted nibbed almonds
½ cup/50 g/2 oz walnuts, finely chopped
a little beaten egg
1 tbsp sugar for dusting

Whisk together the sugar, flour, eggs, mascarpone cheese, cinnamon, nutmeg and lemon zest, and set aside in the refrigerator. Heat the butter in a large non-stick pan, and sweat the apple pieces until tender. Remove from the pan and strain, reserving the liquid in a bowl. Allow the apples to cool.

Put the liquid from the apples into a saucepan and bring to the boil, then reduce until you are left with just 1 tbsp of liquid. Add this to the apples and fold into the egg/mascarpone mixture. Set aside in the refrigerator.

Brush the bottom and sides of an 8½ inch/21.5 cm round flan ring, about 1½ inches/4 cm deep, with melted butter and dust with flour. Roll out a generous half of the pastry and use to line and bottom and sides of the ring. Allow to rest for 30 minutes in the refrigerator. Remove from the refrigerator and line the inside of the ring with greaseproof paper, then fill with baking beans and bake blind in a preheated oven, at 325°F/170°C/gas

mark 3, for 15 minutes. Remove from the oven and allow to cool. Remove the greaseproof paper and baking beans.

Spread the base with the apricot jam and sprinkle the almonds and walnuts on top of the jam. Spread the apple filling on top.

Roll out the remaining pastry slightly larger than the ring, and use this to cover the pie. Seal the edges well and crimp decoratively. Cut off any excess pastry. Cut a small hole in the centre about ¼ inch/½ cm in diameter, then allow to rest in the refrigerator for 15 minutes. Remove from the refrigerator and brush the pastry with a little beaten egg white and sprinkle with a little sugar. Bake in the preheated oven for 1½ hours. If the pastry is browning too quickly, cover with foil.

Remove from the oven and allow to cool. Remove the ring using a sharp knife to loosen the edges. Place on a serving dish and serve slightly warm with an ice-cream of your choice.

*I*n many European countries, 6 December – St Nicholas Day – is celebrated to honour the Patron Saint of Children. As a small boy in my native Switzerland, I can clearly recall waiting with my parents in great anticipation for St Nicholas to arrive. Ears straining, I would hear the front door bell ring, then my aunt opening the door and someone walking up the wooden stairs. A knock on the living room door and there, standing in front of me in his bright red coat with white fur cuffs, was St Nicholas with his mischievous servant Black Peter. He always carried with him a big sack and a book. From the book he would read out all the good things I'd done through the year, and remind me of my transgressions. Then I had to sing a song and was rewarded with a stocking full of nuts, sweets and little chocolates from his big sack. At the same time, as a reminder of my naughtiness, I was handed a birch rod by Black Peter. So in honour of St Nicholas, I've included a children's Christmas Party Menu.

FESTIVE SANDWICH PARCELS

*S*andwiches come in all shapes and sizes. For a St Nicholas party, layer three different types together and tie them up to form a little parcel – one for each child. Make up a few extra and cut these into Christmas shapes using biscuit cutters.

SERVES 8

½ small granary (wholegrain) loaf
½ small brown loaf
½ small white loaf
softened butter

SUGGESTED FILLINGS:
peanut butter, golden syrup and mashed banana
peanut butter, grated apple and chopped raisins
cream cheese and smoked salmon bits
cream cheese, strawberry jam and raisins
egg mayonnaise
tuna mayonnaise and a little ketchup

Put the bread into the freezer for about 2 hours. This will firm it up and make it easier to cut. Prepare 3 different fillings.

Remove the loaves from the freezer and slice into ¼ inch/5 mm slices. Butter each slice thinly on one side only. Sandwich 6 white slices together with one of the fillings. Sandwich 6 brown slices with the second filling and 6 granary (wholegrain) slices with the third filling. Carefully remove the crusts from all sides, then slice each sandwich into 3 fingers. Pile 3 different fingers on top of each other, then tie together with soft red ribbon to form a bow.

Make up the remaining slices using the same or different fillings and cut them into Christmas shapes using biscuit cutters.

VEGETABLE FINGERS WITH AVOCADO DIP

Toddlers and children love to dip food into sauces. This dip is simple, yet delicious. Make extra because parents will enjoy it too! In fact, if you're making it for adults, fold in a couple of finely chopped spring onions and one chopped tomato.

SERVES 8

1 ripe avocado, flesh only
1 tbsp white wine vinegar
3 tbsp sunflower oil
1 tbsp caster (granulated) sugar
½ tsp salt
freshly ground pepper
a selection of raw vegetables, cut into sticks
corn chips

The easiest way to make this is to blend everything in a food processor for 30 seconds.

Alternatively, mash the avocado flesh with a fork and place in a bowl. Add the vinegar, oil, sugar and seasoning. Mix together.

Pile into a bowl and surround with sticks of raw vegetables and crisps.

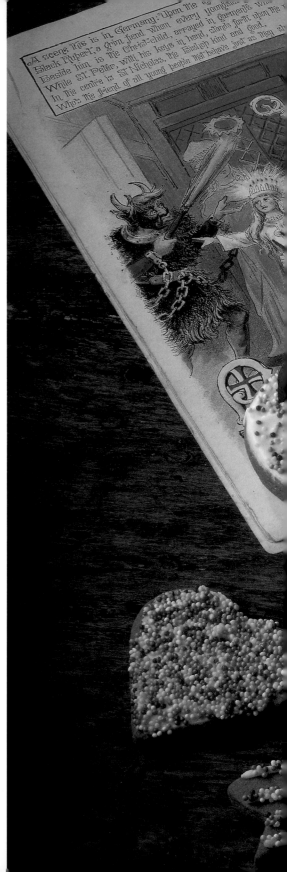

RIGHT: CHRISTMAS TREE COOKIES

CHRISTMAS TREE COOKIES

Spicy biscuits are traditional all over Scandinavia and Europe at Christmas time. These are delicious to eat, and also look pretty hanging on the Christmas tree. They're simple to make, and children will delight in helping to stamp them out and decorate them.

MAKES ABOUT 18–20 COOKIES

¼ cup/75 g/3 oz black treacle (molasses)
½ cup/100 g/4 oz butter
4 cardamom pods, husks split, kernels removed and finely crushed
½ cup/50 g/2 oz caster (granulated) sugar
2 tbsp ground almonds
1⅓ cups/200 g/7 oz plain flour
½ tsp bicarbonate of soda (baking soda)
½ tsp ground cinnamon
½ tsp ground ginger
1 egg yolk

FOR THE ICING:
2 egg whites
3 cups/375 g/13 oz icing (confectioner's) sugar
100s and 1000s (optional)

Melt together the black treacle and butter, then add the crushed cardamom kernels, sugar and almonds. Sift together the flour, bicarbonate (baking soda), cinnamon and ginger, and add this together with the egg yolk. Mix to a dough. Roll into a ball, wrap in clingfilm and chill for 20 minutes.

Place the dough on a floured board and roll to a thickness of ¼ inch/5 mm. Cut out shapes using cutters such as stars, Christmas trees, hearts, etc. Place on lined and greased baking trays and bake in the lower part of the preheated oven at 350°F/180°C/gas mark 4 for about 8 minutes until firm. Remove from the oven and immediately make a hole in each cookie with a skewer. Leave to cool. When cold, move the cookies to a wire tray.

To make the icing, beat the egg whites until slightly thickened. Gradually sift in the icing (confectioner's) sugar, a little at a time, beating well after each addition. Fill the mixture into a piping bag and use to decorate the biscuits. Sprinkle with 100s and 1000s, if liked. When the icing has set, thread a ribbon through each biscuit and tie firmly.

If the cookies are to be eaten, keep them stored in an airtight container for up to one week. Alternatively, they may be used to decorate the Christmas tree.

MERINGUE SNOWMEN

There's a certain mystique about making meringue, but it's actually very easy if you follow these instructions. Piping them into little snowmen will add a touch of festivity to the party table and delight the child in all of us!

MAKES ABOUT 15 SNOWMEN

2 egg whites (cold from the refrigerator)
½ cup/100 g/4 oz caster (granulated) sugar
½ tsp arrowroot
1 pack writing icing e.g. 'Supercook'

Whisk the egg whites until very stiff. Add half the sugar and continue to beat until the mixture holds in stiff peaks. Add the arrowroot to the remaining sugar, then gradually fold this into the mixture.

Line 2 large baking trays with silicone paper. Fill the meringue mixture into a piping bag with a plain round, ½ inch/1 cm nozzle. Put a small blob of meringue under each corner of the paper to hold it secure. Then begin piping. Make one small circle of meringue for the head, about 1 inch/2.5 cm in diameter. Then make another circle of meringue below this, about 1½ inches/4 cm in diameter, for the body. Make 2 small blobs to indicate the feet, then use a small nozzle to pipe the top hat. If you haven't done this before, you might find it easier to draw the shape of the snowman with a pencil on silicone paper before you start piping.

Cook the meringues in the preheated oven at 180°F/90°C/gas mark ¾ for about 1½ hours. Make sure that you do not exceed the temperature given here, or the sugar will turn brown. When the meringues are firm to the touch, turn off the oven and leave them overnight, or until cold.

At this stage, they can be stored in an airtight container for up to 2 weeks. Before serving, use different-coloured writing icing to decorate the snowmen, as shown in the picture.

ICED STAR BISCUITS

These are tasty little star-shaped biscuits that crumble delicately in the mouth. Once the icing has set, they may be stored in an airtight container until required.

MAKES ABOUT 30 COOKIES

½ cup/100 g/4 oz unsalted butter, cold, and cut into cubes
1½ cups/150 g/5oz icing (confectioner's) sugar, sieved
4 egg yolks
a few drops vanilla and lemon essence
1⅓ cups/200 g/7 oz plain flour
⅔ cup/75 g/3 oz ground almonds

FOR THE GLAZE:
the juice of ½ small lemon
4 tbsp (heaped) icing (confectioner's) sugar

Mix together the cold butter and icing sugar. Add the egg yolks, vanilla and lemon essence. Mix in the flour and ground almonds. Knead quickly to a dough, being careful not to over-knead. Wrap the dough in clingfilm and leave in the refrigerator for about 1 hour.

Remove from the refrigerator just before using, and cut into 3 equal portions.

Roll out the dough until about ¼ inch/5 mm thick. Use a cutter to cut out 10 star shapes from each portion. Bake in a preheated oven at 350°F/180°C/gas mark 4 for about 10–12 minutes, then remove from the oven and allow to cool.

Mix together the lemon juice and icing (confectioner's) sugar to form a fairly stiff mixture. When the biscuits are cold, brush with the icing and allow the glaze to dry.

VANILLA ICE-CREAM

This custard-based ice-cream is rich, smooth and speckled with vanilla. With a few changes other delicious variations, such as those suggested below, can easily be made.

SERVES 6 ADULTS

1¼ cups/300 ml/10 fl oz milk
1 vanilla pod, split lengthwise
3 egg yolks
⅓ cup/75 g/3 oz caster (granulated) sugar
1¼ cups/300 ml/10 fl oz double (heavy) cream

Bring the milk and split vanilla pod very slowly to the boil. Remove from the heat, cover and leave to infuse for 30 minutes. Remove the pod and scrape the seeds back into the milk.

Whisk together the egg yolks and sugar until pale and mousse-like. Pour in the vanilla-flavoured milk and strain back into a clean, heavy-based or double saucepan. Heat the custard mixture slowly over gentle heat, stirring all the time, until the mixture thickens enough to coat the back of a wooden spoon. Do not allow to boil. Pour into a large bowl and leave to cool completely.

Whip the cream until thick and fold it thoroughly into the cold custard. The mixture is now ready for freezing. This may either be done in an ice-cream machine or manually in the freezer. If you're using a machine, follow the manufacturer's instructions. Alternatively, place the mixture in a metal bowl in the freezer, pre-set to 'quick freeze'. Leave for about 1 hour or until it is mushy. Then remove from the freezer and whisk thoroughly. Turn the freezer to its normal temperature and return the mixture, in the bowl, to it. Leave for another 1 hour. Again, remove from the freezer and whisk thoroughly. Now transfer to a freezer container, cover and freeze until required. Allow to soften in the refrigerator for 30 minutes before serving.

VARIATIONS

CINNAMON: Replace the vanilla pod with a stick of cinnamon. When removing the stick, discard and add ¼ tsp of ground cinnamon to the milk.

WALNUT: Omit the vanilla pod. Replace the sugar with soft brown sugar. Add 1 cup/4 oz/100g of finely chopped walnuts to the mixture when half frozen.

CARAMEL CRUNCH: Omit the vanilla pod. Replace the sugar with soft dark brown sugar. Add 1½ cups/6 oz/175g butter almond chocolate bars (DIME bars), chopped, to the mixture when half frozen.

LEFT: MERINGUE SNOWMEN

SANTA SAUCE

The sweet sharpness of this sauce accompanies the rich ice-cream superbly. Children are sure to be thrilled when they know it's Santa's favourite! Alternatively, to make a delicious raspberry ripple ice-cream, fold half of it into the almost-frozen vanilla ice-cream to form ribbons, then freeze until firm.

MAKES 2¼ CUPS/500 ML/18 FL OZ

9 oz/250 g fresh ripe raspberries
2½ cups/250 g/9 oz icing (confectioner's) sugar
8½ tbsp/125 ml/4½ fl oz water

Mix together all the ingredients in a saucepan. Bring slowly to the boil and simmer for 2 minutes. Liquidize the mixture in a food processor or blender, and pass through a sieve. Allow to cool or serve warm.

The sweetness of raspberries can vary. If you wish to sweeten the sauce, shake a little icing (confectioner's) sugar into it towards the end.

*I*n Scandinavia, the Christmas festivities start on 13 December – St Lucia's Day – when by tradition the eldest daughter wakes the family up to Santa Lucia Buns and steaming coffee. Dressed in white, with a red sash at her waist and a wreath of greenery holding seven lighted candles on her head, she also sings the Santa Lucia song. This is to honour Lucia, a Christian maid martyred in the fourth century. According to legend, prior to her death, she took food to feed Christians hiding in the catacombs each night. To have her hands free, she carried the lights in her hair. This story was passed to the Christian Vikings who envisaged her surounded by a halo of light. This beautiful tradition lies behind my menu for a St Lucia Breakfast. It can be achieved without too much effort and is sure to give great enjoyment to your family and friends over the festive period.

MELON AND CLEMENTINES IN STAR ANISE AND GINGER SYRUP

A refreshing start to the day: prepare the syrup the day before and simply pour it over the fruit the next morning. To garnish use any variety of berries or a few black grapes.

SERVES 4

4 clementines (clementine oranges)
½ honeydew melon, peeled and deseeded

FOR THE SYRUP:
½ cup/100 g/4 oz caster (granulated) sugar
3 slices fresh ginger, peeled and cut into ⅛ inch/3 mm rings
juice of ½ lime
1 star anise
1 cup/250 ml/8 fl oz water

TO GARNISH:
fresh berries such as raspberries or strawberries
fresh mint, icing (confectioner's) sugar

To make the syrup, put all the ingredients into a saucepan, place over gentle heat and allow the sugar to dissolve. Bring to the boil and simmer for 2–3 minutes, then pass through a sieve and allow to cool.

Plunge the clementines into boiling water for about 3 minutes, then refresh in cold water and peel. Divide into segments and put into a medium-sized bowl. Cut the half melon lengthwise into 3 pieces and then crosswise into ⅛ inch/3 mm slices, and add to the clementine segments. Pour the syrup over and allow to macerate for 30 minutes.

Serve in a glass bowl or spoon on to plates and garnish with the fresh raspberries, strawberries or other berries. Add the mint and sprinkle with a little icing (confectioner's) sugar.

BAKED SMOKED SALMON OMELETTES WITH SOURED DILL SAUCE

A variation on the classic combination of smoked salmon and eggs, this is delicious. Be sure not to overcook the omelettes. They should be golden on the outside but still a little moist in the middle.

SERVES 4

FOR THE OMELETTE:
2 tbsp vegetable oil
2 tbsp/25 g/1 oz butter
12 eggs
6 oz/175 g smoked salmon, cut into fine strips
2 tbsp chives, chopped
salt and freshly ground white pepper
1 tsp spring onion, finely chopped

FOR THE SAUCE:
1 cup/200 ml/7 fl oz soured (sour) cream
1 tbsp fresh dill, finely chopped
2 tbsp salmon roe
½ tsp grated horseradish cream
salt and freshly ground pepper

To make the sauce, mix all the ingredients together and set aside.

To make the omelettes, start by dividing the ingredients into 4 portions. Heat a quarter of the vegetable oil in a 6–8 inch/15–20 cm, non-stick pan. Lightly whisk 3 eggs. Add to the pan and stir with a wooden spoon. Then add a quarter of the smoked salmon, spring onion and chives. Stir, then cook slowly over medium heat without stirring until slightly brown on the base.

Turn the omelette and brown it on the other side but make sure that it is still moist inside. Turn upside-down on a plate and keep warm. Repeat the process until you have made 4 omelettes. Serve the omelettes with the soured dill sauce.

RIGHT: BAKED SMOKED SALMON OMELETTE WITH SOURED DILL SAUCE

St Lucia Buns

In Sweden, *lussekake* are served, early in the morning, on 13 December. The traditional shape is that of two 'S's crossed over, but it's fun to twist them into any shape that catches your imagination. If you plan to serve them for breakfast, I suggest making them the day before and reheating them gently to serve warm with plenty of butter.

MAKES 12 BUNS

4 tbsp/165 g/5½ oz sugar
4 tsp dried active baking yeast
½ cup/100 ml/4 fl oz tepid water
⅔ cup/150 ml/5 fl oz single (light) cream
3 eggs
½ cup/100 g/4 oz unsalted butter, cubed

1 tsp saffron threads, crumbled
1¼ lb/550 g strong white bread flour
generous ⅓ cup/65 g/2½ oz sultanas (sultana raisins)
⅔ cup/75 g/3 oz ground almonds
1 tsp salt
about ¼ cup raisins to decorate

Dissolve 1 tsp of the sugar in the tepid water. Sprinkle the dried yeast over this and whisk well. Cover with clingfilm. Allow the mixture to stand in a warm draught-free place for about 10–15 minutes until frothy.

Meanwhile, bring the cream to the boil and remove from the heat. Add the remaining sugar, butter and saffron. Allow the butter to melt and the mixture to reach room temperature.

Sift the flour and salt into a large bowl. Add the ground almonds and sultanas. Make a well in the centre. Whisk together the yeast and cream mixtures. Then add 2 of the eggs, lighly beaten. Now pour this liquid into the flour and gradually mix together. Start by using a wooden spoon, then use your hands to form a soft dough. Turn on to a lightly floured board and knead for 5–10 minutes, until smooth and elastic. Place in a lightly buttered bowl and cover with a damp towel. Leave to rise in a warm, draught-free place for about 1½ hours.

Turn the dough again on to a lightly floured board and knock back. Divide into 24 pieces.

Roll each of these into a 'rope' about 8 inches/20 cm long. Form each rope into an 'S' shape, coiling the ends into a snail shape. Place two 'S' shapes diagonally across each other, pressing lightly in the centre. Place a raisin in the centre of each coil.

Place all the buns on a large baking tray, lined with greased silicone paper. Cover with a damp tea towel. Leave for about 40 minutes, until doubled in size. Whisk the remaining egg lightly and brush over each bun. Bake in a preheated oven at 350°F/180°C/gas mark 4 for about 12 minutes until golden brown. Remove and allow to cool slightly on a wire rack before serving. Alternatively, cool completely, store in an airtight container overnight and reheat gently the following morning.

'Silent Night, Holy Night.' In Austria, as in many other European countries, Christmas is traditionally a personal affair. On Christmas Eve, the family gathers around a fir tree decorated with candles, biscuits and other ornaments. The centre of attraction is an ornamental nativity scene very carefully carved out of wood and passed down from generation to generation.

Outside, *turmblasen,* which is the sound of brass instruments being played from the main church steeple or city tower, may be heard. It is traditional to serve a dinner of carp – fried, braised in beer or simply poached – and at midnight, matins are celebrated throughout Austria.

CARP IN BEER

Carp is used widely in Austria and Germany. The bitterness of the beer and the sweetness of the gingerbread in this recipe give a robust flavour to the sauce. Carp needs to be well rinsed in fresh water before being cooked.

SERVES 4

2 medium carp fillets
salt and freshly ground pepper
2 tbsp vegetable oil

FOR THE SAUCE:
2 tbsp/25 g/1 oz butter
1 shallot, finely chopped
½ cup/100 ml/4 fl oz white wine
1 cup/250 ml/8 fl oz fish stock
½ cup/100 ml/4 fl oz brown ale
3 fairly thick slices gingerbread (spice cake), cut into cubes
salt and freshly ground pepper
1 tbsp finely chopped chives

Pat dry the carp fillets with kitchen towel, then season with salt and pepper.

Heat the oil in a non-stick pan and add the fillets. Brown quickly on both sides, then place in an ovenproof dish.

To make the sauce, heat the butter in a saucepan and add the shallot. Sweat until translucent but not coloured. Add the white wine, bring to the boil and reduce rapidly until halved in quantity. Add the fish stock and bring to the boil, then add the beer and gingerbread. Mix together and return to the boil. Simmer for 5 minutes. Adjust the seasoning. Pass the mixture through a sieve on to the carp in the serving dish. Cover with a lid and cook for about 10–15 minutes in a preheated oven at 375°F/190°C/gas mark 5.

Remove from oven, sprinkle with chopped chives and serve.

ROAST LOIN OF VENISON WITH PUMPKIN AND WILD MUSHROOMS

Roast pumpkin is one of my favourite vegetable accompaniments with a traditional roast. Here I have combined it with succulent loin of venison, and have given it a final flourish of wild mushrooms for a hearty winter flavour.

SERVES 4

3 tbsp vegetable oil
1½ lb/700 g loin of venison, boned and rolled
2 cloves of garlic, not peeled
12 oz/350 g pumpkin, peeled, deseeded and cut into
½ inch/1 cm cubes
2 cups/125 g/4 oz wild mushrooms, the large ones quartered
1 tsp chopped chives
1 tsp vegetable oil
rosemary to garnish

FOR THE SAUCE:
2 tbsp/25 g/1 oz butter
½ shallot, finely chopped
½ cup/100 ml/4 fl oz red wine
1 tsp redcurrant jelly
1 cup/250 ml/8 fl oz chicken stock
salt and freshly ground white pepper
2 tsp cornflour (cornstarch) mixed with 1 tbsp water

Heat the butter gently in a saucepan. Add the shallots and sweat until translucent but not coloured. Add the wine and bring rapidly to the boil, then reduce to half its quantity. Add the redcurrant jelly and stock, and boil rapidly, again reducing to half its quantity. Add the cornflour (cornstarch) to thicken, and season with salt and pepper. Strain the sauce through a sieve into a saucepan, and set aside.

To cook the venison, place 2 tbsp of the oil in a roasting tray large enough to hold the venison and pumpkin comfortably. Heat the oil for a few minutes in a preheated oven at 375°F/190°C/gas mark 5. Season the venison with salt and pepper, and place on the tray together with the garlic. Brown quickly on all sides in the oven. After 5 minutes, add the pumpkin pieces to the tray and continue roasting for another 7 minutes or so (depending on the thickness of the meat), until the venison is medium-cooked and tender.

Remove the venison from the tray and allow it to rest for 5 minutes. Leave the pumpkin in the oven until cooked, then remove from the tray with a perforated spoon and place in a flat dish. Keep somewhere warm.

Heat the remaining vegetable oil in a non-stick pan. When it is very hot, add the mushrooms and brown quickly. Add the roasted pumpkin, toss and season with salt and freshly ground white pepper. Add the chives and spoon the mixture equally on the plates. Place slices of venison on top and garnish with the rosemary. Heat the sauce and serve separately.

RIGHT: ROAST LOIN OF VENISON WITH PUMPKIN AND WILD MUSHROOMS

CRANBERRY AND BAKED PEAR
PANCAKES WITH CALVADOS CREAM

Everything for these pancakes can easily be prepared in advance, but if the filling is cold when they are placed in the oven, allow a little longer for it to heat through.

MAKES 4 X 9 INCH/23 CM PANCAKES

½ cup/65 g/2½ oz plain flour
⅔ cup/150 ml/5 fl oz milk
1 egg, lightly beaten
½ tsp oil
butter to grease the pan

½ cup/100 ml/4 fl oz white wine
1 tbsp caster (granulated) sugar
¼ cinnamon stick
1 tbsp apricot jam
icing (confectioner's) sugar

FOR THE FILLING:
¾ cup/75 g/3 oz fresh cranberries
4 William pears, peeled and cored
2 tbsp/25 g/1 oz butter
juice of 1 orange

TO SERVE:
crème anglaise or custard
calvados
berries, and mint or holly leaves to garnish

To make the pancakes, place the flour in a mixing bowl. Blend in the milk, beaten egg and oil. Cover the bowl and allow to rest for 10 minutes.

Brush a non-stick pan with melted butter. Add a quarter of the pancake batter (about 4 tbsp), and swirl the pan round so that the batter coats it evenly. Cook until the underside is golden, then turn and cook the other side. Remove from the pan and set aside. Do not lay the pancakes on top of each other or they will stick.

To make the filling, cook the cranberries in boiling water for 2 minutes. Drain and set aside.

Cut the pears into quarters, then cut into ¼ inch/5 mm pieces. Heat the butter and sweat the pieces of pear and cranberries for about 1 minute without colouring. Add the white wine, orange juice, cinnamon stick and sugar. Bring to the boil and cook until the pear is tender. Strain the liquid through a sieve into a pan. Set aside the pear and cranberry mixture, and remove the cinnamon stick. Bring the liquid to the boil, add the apricot jam and boil until reduced by half, then mix together with the pear and cranberry mixture.

Place the pancakes in front of you and divide the filling equally into the centre of each pancake. Fold in about 1 inch/2.5 cm on both sides, then roll each into a cigar shape. Place in an ovenproof dish and sprinkle with the icing (confectioner's) sugar. Place under a preheated grill to brown. Garnish with fresh berries, and mint or holly leaves, and serve with crème anglaise or custard, flavoured to taste with 1 or 2 tbsp calvados.

LEFT: CRANBERRY AND BAKED PEAR PANCAKES WITH CALVADOS CREAM

On Christmas Eve in France, after attending Mass in church, it is customary to return home to enjoy the main Christmas meal – the *réveillon*. This may include a starter of foie gras or oysters, followed by ham, goose, turkey or capon, and often a dish of black pudding, and, finally, the bûche de Noël, or Yule log. The origins of this famous cake lie in the burning of a Yule log, which was an annual pagan custom, later adopted by the Christians, found right across Europe. An enormous log would be dragged into the equally large hearth, then blessed and welcomed with a splash of wine. It would then be lit with a piece of the log reserved from the previous year and, to ensure good luck in the coming year, carefully tended so that it burned through the twelve days of Christmas. Today, few of us have fireplaces large enough to continue this tradition but it still lives on, symbolized in France by this delicious chocolate version of the log.

Escalope of Sea Bass With Lime and Champagne Sauce

*C*hampagne and sea bass are both particular favourites of mine, and, coupled with the caramelized zest of lime in this recipe, they make a winning combination.

Serves 4

1 tsp finely grated lime zest
½ tsp icing (confectioner's) sugar
2 tbsp vegetable oil
1 lb 6 oz/600 g fillet of sea bass, cut into 4 portions
coriander (cilantro) to garnish

For the Sauce:
2 tbsp/25 g/1 oz unsalted butter
½ shallot, finely chopped

2 tbsp/25 ml/1 fl oz white wine
2 tbsp/25 ml/1 fl oz dry champagne
½ cup plus 2 tbsp/150 ml/5 fl oz double (heavy) cream
½ cup/100 ml/4 fl oz fish stock
salt and freshly ground white pepper
2 tsp chopped coriander (cilantro) leaves
¼ tsp chopped basil leaves

Mix together the lime zest and sugar. Put on a baking tray. Place under the grill on the bottom level until caramelized. Remove immediately and allow to cool. Remove from the tray with a metal spatula, crush into small pieces with the back of a knife, and set aside. Heat the butter in a saucepan and sweat the shallots until translucent. Add the white wine and champagne. Bring to the boil and reduce by half. Add the fish stock and return to the boil. Reduce again by half. Add the cream and simmer until creamy. Pass the sauce through a sieve into a clean saucepan and bring to the boil. Season, and set aside. Heat the oil in a non-stick pan and season the sea bass. Brown on both sides and place on a baking tray. Bake in a preheated oven at 325°F/170°C/gas mark 3 for 6–8 minutes or until cooked. Remove, place skin side up on a serving dish and keep warm. Bring the sauce back to the boil, add the leaves, and the caramelized lime zest. Pour the sauce around the fish and serve, garnished with coriander (cilantro).

ABOVE: ESCALOPE OF SEA BASS WITH LIME AND CHAMPAGNE SAUCE

GINGERED CHICKEN BREASTS

Based on the classic 'coq au vin', this recipe has a ginger twist. It also uses only breasts, which allows a shorter cooking time. For the best results, however, ensure that they are not overcooked.

SERVES 4

4 large chicken breasts
salt and freshly ground pepper
white flour to dust the chicken
4 tsp vegetable oil

FOR THE SAUCE:
2 tbsp/25 g/1 oz butter
2 shallots, finely chopped
½ clove garlic, finely chopped
1 small carrot, diced
¼ tsp finely chopped fresh ginger
½ cup/100 ml/4 fl oz red wine
½ cup/100 ml/4 fl oz medium sherry

½ cup/100 ml/4 fl oz chicken stock
½ tsp cornflour (cornstarch), dissolved in a little red wine
2 tbsp double (heavy) cream
1 cup/50 g/2 oz button mushrooms, finely chopped at the last moment
salt and freshly ground white pepper

TO GARNISH:
1 tbsp/15 oz/½ oz butter
8 small onions, cooked in salted water, refreshed and drained
8 sugar snap peas, cooked in salted water, refreshed and drained
8 medium-sized button mushrooms, cut in half

Season the chicken with salt and pepper, and dust it lightly with flour. Heat the oil in a non-stick frying pan, and brown the chicken on all sides, then remove and transfer it into an oven-proof dish. Set aside.

To prepare the sauce, take the pan used to brown the chicken, pour off the remaining oil and add the butter. Add the shallots, carrot, garlic and ginger, and sweat until translucent but not coloured. Add the red wine and boil rapidly, reducing the liquid to half its quantity. Add the sherry and return to the boil, reducing again to half its quantity. Add the chicken stock and bring to the boil.

Pour the sauce over the chicken breasts and return, covered, to the preheated oven at 350°F/180°C/gas mark 4 for about 10–12 minutes until the chicken is cooked. Then remove from the oven. Transfer the chicken breasts to a serving dish and set aside to keep warm. Pass the sauce through a sieve into a saucepan, bring to the boil and reduce the liquid to half its quantity (skim if necessary). Season with salt and pepper.

Whisk in the dissolved cornflour (cornstarch) and bring to the boil. Add the cream and the finely chopped mushrooms. Simmer for 1 minute, then remove from the heat and set aside.

To finish, heat a non-stick pan and add the butter and onions. Brown them slightly and add the button mushrooms and sugar snap peas. Season well. Bring the sauce to the boil and pour over the chicken breasts. Use a perforated spoon to place the garnish on top, and serve.

NUTTY WILD RICE

Wild rice has a deliciously nutty texture and flavour. Here I've teamed it with brown rice for flavour and toasted pecan nuts for extra crunch.

SERVES 4–6

3 cups/700 ml/24 fl oz chicken stock
½ cup/100 g/4 oz wild rice
2 tbsp/25 g/1 oz unsalted butter
½ cup/100 g/4 oz brown rice
½ cup/50 g/2 oz pecan nuts, coarsely chopped
4 tbsp finely chopped fresh parsley
salt and freshly ground white pepper

Bring the chicken stock to the boil in a large saucepan. Add the wild rice and half the butter, then return to the boil. Stir and cover, and allow to simmer very gently for 10 minutes.

Add the brown rice and stir gently. Return to the boil and cover. Allow to simmer gently for another 45 minutes, then remove the lid and leave for another 5 minutes.

Meanwhile, melt the remaining butter in a frying pan and toast the chopped pecans a little. Fold into the rice with the parsley. Toss gently with a fork and transfer to a serving bowl.

BROCCOLI PURÉE WITH LEEK

A colourful vegetable purée. This is an excellent accompaniment that contrasts well with the crunchiness of the Nutty Wild Rice. Thinned with a little vegetable stock, it also makes a tasty soup.

SERVES 4

1 lb/450 g broccoli, trimmed, stems peeled and
roughly chopped
1 cup/250 ml/8 fl oz crème fraîche (or sour cream)
2 tbsp vegetable oil
1 shallot, finely chopped
½ clove garlic, crushed
1 medium-sized leek, green leaves removed, finely cubed
salt and freshly ground white pepper
freshly grated nutmeg

Bring a large pan of water to the boil and cook the broccoli until tender. Strain through a sieve, reserving ¼ cup/50 ml/2 fl oz of the cooking liquid. Put the broccoli into a food processor and add the crème fraîche (or sour cream). Purée thoroughly and set aside.

Heat the vegetable oil in a medium-sized pan, and add the shallots and garlic. Sweat until the shallots are translucent but not coloured. Add the leek and sweat for a further 1 minute.

Add the reserved vegetable stock, cover with a lid and simmer over medium heat until the leek is tender. Then remove the lid and add the broccoli purée. Heat through, season with salt, pepper and ground nutmeg, and serve in a hot serving dish.

YULE LOG

The bûche de Noël comes in many guises. Traditionally, it is a chocolate roll, filled with chestnut purée and decorated to look like a log. This recipe is rich and quite delicious.

SERVES 10

5 oz/150 g plain chocolate,
    chopped finely
¼ cup/50 ml/2 fl oz water
5 eggs, separated
1 cup plus 2 tbsp/225 g/8 oz
    caster (granulated) sugar
sifted icing (confectioner's)
    sugar

FOR THE FILLING:
4 tbsp double (heavy) cream
1 tbsp milk
1 x 9 oz/250 g can sweetened
    chestnut purée

FOR THE ICING:
⅓ cup/75 g/3 oz caster
    (granulated) sugar
5 tbsp water
2 egg yolks
⅔ cup/150 g/5 oz unsalted
    butter, softened
2 oz/50 g plain chocolate,
    chopped finely
sifted icing (confectioner's)
    sugar
holly leaves or marzipan
    mushrooms to decorate

Melt the chocolate in the water over gentle heat, taking care not to overheat the mixture. Remove and allow to cool slightly. Combine the egg yolks and sugar in a large bowl and whisk until the mixture is thick, mousse-like and pale. Add the melted chocolate and mix thoroughly.

Next ensure that your whisk and bowl are absolutely clean and dry, and whisk the egg whites until they form soft peaks. Fold the whites into the chocolate mixture, ensuring that they are thoroughly combined. Spread the mixture evenly into a 12 x 10 inch/30 x 25 cm Swiss roll tin, lined with greased silicone paper. Bake in a preheated oven at 350°F/180°C/gas mark 4 for about 12 minutes, until it is just firm to the touch.

LEFT: YULE LOG

Remove from the oven and cover with a clean, damp tea towel. Leave in a cool place (not the refrigerator) for at least 4 hours or overnight, until cold.

Place a sheet of greaseproof or silicone paper, slightly larger than the tin, on a work surface. Dust well with sifted icing (confectioner's) sugar. Remove the cloth from the roll, loosen the paper around the edges and carefully turn it out on to the paper. Peel off the lining paper.

To prepare the filling, whisk the cream and milk together until stiff, then fold in the chestnut purée. Spread this evenly over the base. Using the paper as a guide, gently roll up the log lengthwise. Don't worry if it cracks – the icing will cover it all.

To ice it, gently dissolve the sugar in 4 tbsp of the water. Increase the heat and boil steadily for 3–4 minutes until you reach the thread stage (225°F/110°C). If you don't have a sugar thermometer, test this by dipping the back of two wooden spoons into the syrup and waiting a second before gently pulling them apart. At the correct stage, thin threads will form between the spoons.

Place the yolks in a bowl, and whisking continuously, pour on the syrup in a thin stream. Whisk until the mixture is thick and cold, then gradually add the softened butter. Gently melt the chocolate in the remaining 1 tbsp of water until smooth, then beat it into the syrup.

To finish off the log, cut a piece diagonally off each end of the log about 2 inches/5 cm at the widest point. Place one piece on one side of the log and the other on the other side as 'branches'. Spread the chocolate icing over the log. Using a fork, scrape it lightly to resemble woody bark, and swirl in circles at the ends to resemble the inside of a log.

Using a palette knife, gently lift it on to a serving plate. Garnish with holly leaves and/or mushrooms made out of marzipan.

*C*hristmas in England today owes much to the Victorians, and in particular to Charles Dickens and Prince Albert. Their love of festivity and good food has resulted in the warmest of yuletides. These customs continue each year at the Dorchester, where festivities start at the beginning of December and reach their climax on Christmas Day. In the kitchens, thousands of chestnuts are peeled and cooked, hundreds of turkeys are roasted, and our delicious puddings are flamed with brandy. Lunch at the Dorchester is kept traditional, as is this menu for you to prepare at home.

QUENELLES OF SMOKED SALMON

*W*ith so much do on Christmas Day, a simple starter is called for. Eye-catching, with a unique taste, this is a personal favourite of mine.

SERVES 4

11 oz/300 g smoked salmon finely diced
1 shallot, very finely chopped
1 tsp very finely chopped chives
2 tsp mild white wine vinegar
2 tsp walnut oil
1 tsp sunflower oil
salt and freshly ground white pepper
1 squeeze lime juice

FOR THE SAUCE:
¾ cup plus 2 tbsp/200 ml/7 fl oz soured (sour) cream
1 tbsp salmon roe
salt and freshly ground pepper

FOR THE GARNISH:
a selection of salad leaves, such as corn salad, celery leaves
and lollo rosso, fresh dill

In a bowl, mix together the smoked salmon, shallots and chives. In another small bowl, mix together the vinegar and oils, then add gently to the salmon mixture. Season with salt and pepper, and add lime juice to taste. Set aside.

To prepare the sauce, mix together the soured cream and salmon roe. Season with salt and pepper, then pour into a sauceboat and set aside.

Finally, to make the quenelles, you will need 2 dessertspoons. Heap 1 spoon full with the salmon mixture, and then use the second spoon to shape the mixture into a quenelle shape. Place 3 quenelles on each plate and garnish with the salad leaves and dill. Serve the sauce separately.

ABOVE: QUENELLES OF SMOKED SALMON

TRADITIONAL TURKEY WITH CHESTNUT STUFFING

As I said earlier, a fresh bird is always best. Both bird and stuffing should be at room temperature before proceeding. This is a very traditionally British method of roasting, which will result in a flavourful succulent bird.

SERVES 8

*10–12 lb/4.5–5.5 kg oven-ready turkey
with giblets
1 quantity chestnut stuffing (see page 52)
1 onion
½ cup/125 g/4 oz butter, softened*

*10 oz/275 g streaky bacon
salt and freshly ground black pepper
cocktail-sized chipolata sausages and
rashers of rindless streaky bacon,
stretched, halved and rolled up, to garnish*

*For the Gravy:
turkey giblets, excluding liver
2½ cups/600 ml/1 pint chicken stock
1 tbsp cornflour (cornstarch) or arrowroot
2 tbsp dry sherry*

Remove the giblets from the turkey and keep refrigerated until required. Wash the turkey well and dry both inside and out with kitchen towel.

Loosely fill the neck cavity with the stuffing, pushing it gently up beneath the skin towards the breast. Pull the flap of skin under the bird and secure with a skewer. Salt the body cavity. Weigh the dressed bird. Cut the onion in 4 lengthwise and place inside.

Cut 2 sheets of foil – each piece should be large enough to wrap generously right round the turkey. Lay these on top of each other on a clean work surface. Place the turkey breast side up on the foil. Smother the breasts, legs and thighs with the butter and sprinkle with salt and freshly ground pepper. Lastly, cover the breast, legs and thighs with the overlapping bacon rashers. Now wrap the bird loosely in the foil. Ensure that it is sealed. Gently lift the parcel into the roasting tray and place in a preheated oven at 425°F/220°C/gas mark 7.

After 30 minutes, reduce the oven temperature to 325°F/170°C/gas mark 3 and cook for a further 3½–4¼ hours according to size. About 30 minutes before the end of the cooking time, remove the turkey from the oven and increase the temperature to 425°F/220°C/gas mark 7 again. Carefully

remove the turkey from the foil, replacing it and the juices back into the roasting tray. Remove the bacon from the bird. Return the turkey to the oven for a final 30 minutes to brown evenly.

To check that the turkey is cooked, pierce the thigh with a skewer – the juices must run clear with no trace of pink. When it is cooked, remove the turkey from the oven, place it on a warm platter, and cover with foil. Allow to rest in a warm place for 30–45 minutes before carving with a sharp knife.

Put the chipolata sausages and bacon rolls in another roasting tray (secure the bacon rolls with toothpicks so that they don't unravel). Pop into the bottom of the oven and cook for 15 minutes, turning once.

To start the gravy, place the giblets in the original roasting tray and return to the oven. After about 20 minutes, remove the giblets from the oven and pour off the excess fat. Place the tray on top of the cooker over medium heat and pour over the chicken stock. Allow to simmer for 10 minutes. Dissolve the cornflour (cornstarch) or arrowroot in a little water and whisk it in. Allow to simmer for a few minutes to thicken. Strain, add the sherry, taste and adjust the seasoning. Keep warm until required.

LEFT: TRADITIONAL TURKEY WITH CHESTNUT STUFFING

CHESTNUT STUFFING

No Christmas bird is complete without a stuffing. My choice is to combine chestnuts with pork meat and bacon. It's very traditional, with a hearty flavour and lots of fatty juices which help to keep the turkey moist. It can be made the day before and refrigerated overnight.

TO STUFF A 10–12 LB/4.5–5.5 KG TURKEY

¼ cup/50 g/2 oz butter
4 oz/125 g streaky bacon, rind removed and finely chopped
1 onion, finely chopped
3 cloves garlic, crushed
2 cups/125 g/4 oz mushrooms, coarsely chopped
8 oz/225 g unsweetened chestnut purée (or whole, peeled and cooked chestnuts, roughly chopped)
1 tbsp finely chopped oregano, thyme or parsley
8 oz/225 g pork sausagemeat
1 egg, lightly beaten
salt and freshly ground pepper

Melt the butter and add the bacon, onion and garlic. Cook over gentle heat for about 5 minutes until the onions are soft but not coloured. Add the mushrooms, stir gently, and leave for another 2 minutes. Remove from the heat and allow to cool.

Place all the remaining ingredients in a large mixing bowl. Add the entire contents of the pan and mix thoroughly. Season to taste.

Cover and refrigerate until required. Allow it to reach room temperature before using.

ROAST PHEASANT WITH WILD MUSHROOMS

If you want a break from tradition, try this hearty winter dish. For the best results it should be served with the pheasant slightly pink. Accompany with bread sauce.

SERVES 4

4 tbsp vegetable oil
2 pheasants, cleaned
salt and freshly ground pepper
½ cinnamon stick
4 bacon rashers, cut crosswise into ½ inch/2 cm strips
12 small silverskin onions, boiled and refreshed
2 cups/100 g/4 oz wild mushrooms, large ones halved or quartered

FOR THE SAUCE:
2 tbsp vegetable oil
1 shallot, finely chopped
½ clove garlic, crushed
2¼ cups/300 ml/½ pint chicken stock
½ cup/100 ml/4 fl oz soured (sour) cream
1 tbsp cornflour (cornstarch)
salt and freshly ground pepper
1 tsp chopped fresh parsley

Heat the oil in a roasting pan and quickly brown each pheasant on all sides. Then season and place, breast side up, in the roasting pan together with the cinnamon stick. Roast in a preheated oven at 350°F/180°C/gas mark 4 for 25–30 minutes, basting constantly, until cooked but still pink.

Meanwhile, to make the sauce, heat the vegetable oil in a saucepan and add the shallot and garlic. Sweat until the shallots are translucent but not coloured.

Add the chicken stock, bring to the boil and simmer for 5 minutes. Add the soured cream and return to the boil. In a bowl, dissolve the cornflour (cornstarch) in 2 tbsp of water. Whisk it into the stock and simmer until thickened. Season, then remove from the heat and put to one side.

When the pheasants are cooked, remove them from the roasting pan and allow to rest in a warm place for about 10 minutes.

Meanwhile, heat a non-stick pan and add the strips of bacon and the cooked onions. Brown the bacon on all sides and heat the onions through. Add the wild mushrooms and sauté for 1 minute. Pass the sauce through a sieve into the bacon and mushroom mixture. Adjust the seasoning and put to one side.

To make it easier to carve the birds, remove the wishbones, cut them in half, and place on a serving dish. Add the chopped parsley to the hot sauce, and pour around the pheasants.

BREAD SAUCE

Traditional with Christmas turkey, this is also delicious with chicken, pheasant and grouse. We inherited this recipe from Scotland. A good bread sauce is creamy and well spiced.

SERVES 8

12 cloves
1 large onion, peeled and halved lengthwise
¼ tsp freshly grated nutmeg
1 bay leaf
5 black peppercorns
1¼ cups/300 ml/½ pint full-cream (whole) milk
¾ cup/150 ml/¼ pint chicken stock
¾ cup/150 ml/¼ pint single (light) cream
2 cups/100 g/4 oz fresh breadcrumbs
¼ cup/50 g/2 oz butter, at room temperature
salt and freshly ground black pepper

Stick the cloves into the onion halves. Place these, together with the nutmeg, bay leaf and peppercorns in a pan. Pour over the milk, stock and cream. Place over a moderate heat and bring to the boil. Then remove from the heat, cover with a lid and leave the flavours to infuse for at least 1 hour. Pass through a fine sieve.

About 30 minutes before serving, add the breadcrumbs and return to the lowest heat possible. Cook uncovered, stirring occasionally, until the breadcrumbs have thickened the sauce to a creamy consistency. Just before serving, whisk in the butter, salt and pepper. Taste, adjust the seasoning, and pour into a warm serving bowl.

OVEN-ROAST POTATOES

These are best left in the oven until just before serving. Once you have taken them out of the oven, never cover them or they'll go soggy.

SERVES 4

24 medium-sized new potatoes
vegetable oil
salt and freshly ground pepper
sprig of fresh rosemary

Bring some water to the boil in a saucepan large enough to hold the potatoes easily. In the meantime, peel the potatoes and, when the water is boiling, drop them into it and allow to boil for 3–4 minutes. Drain in a colander, then spread on a tray, making sure they are in one layer. Their own heat will make any excess water evaporate. Allow the potatoes to cool.

Heat a roasting or baking tray, large enough to hold the potatoes in a single layer, in the oven. Add the vegetable oil, and when it is hot add the potatoes and rosemary. Roast in a pre-heated oven at 400°F/200°C/gas mark 6 for about 15 minutes, depending on their size, until cooked, crisp and golden brown. Transfer from the oven to a serving dish with a perforated spoon, season with salt and serve immediately.

SHREDDED BRUSSELS SPROUTS IN CREAM

The creamy sauce with a hint of nutmeg makes magic of this understated vegetable. This is a welcome alternative to plain boiled sprouts.

SERVES 4

1 lb 5 oz/600 g small Brussels sprouts
2 tbsp vegetable oil
2 shallots, finely chopped
½ cup/100 ml/4 fl oz vegetable stock
¾ cup plus 2 tbsp/200 ml/7 fl oz double (heavy) cream
salt and freshly ground white pepper
2 pinches grated nutmeg
1 tsp finely chopped parsley

Prepare the Brussels sprouts by removing all the dark green outer leaves. Wash and drain, then cut them in half lengthwise, then crosswise into fine strips.

Heat the vegetable oil in a large saucepan, add the shallots and sweat until translucent but not coloured. Add the vegetable stock and bring to the boil rapidly. Add the cream and return to the boil.

Add the shredded sprouts and stir well. Bring to the boil, cover with a lid and simmer for about 5–10 minutes or until cooked.

Remove the sprouts with a perforated spoon and place them in a serving dish. Bring the liquid to the boil and simmer until a creamy consistency is obtained. Season with salt, pepper and nutmeg. Pour over the sprouts, sprinkle with parsley and serve.

DORCHESTER CHRISTMAS PUDDING

This recipe needs to be made well in advance to allow the flavours to develop. For this reason I have included it together with others in Menu 1. You will find it on page 15.

BRANDY SAUCE

Delicious with Christmas pudding! If you prefer Rum Sauce, substitute rum for the brandy and add a generous grating of nutmeg.

SERVES 8

4 egg yolks
2 tbsp cornflour (cornstarch)
2 tbsp demerara (granulated) sugar
2½ cups/600 ml/1 pint single (light) cream
3–4 tbsp brandy

In a small bowl, mix together the egg yolks, cornflour (cornstarch) and sugar. Whisk lightly to combine. Pour the cream into the top of a double boiler. Add the egg mixture. Stir continuously over simmering water until the sauce is the consistency of custard, then add the brandy. Pour into a serving jug and cover with a small circle of greaseproof/silicone paper to stop a skin forming. Keep warm.

MINCE PIES

Today mince pies are round, but originally they were oval to represent the crib. You are supposed to eat twelve – to bring good luck for each month of the year. A good excuse if ever I heard one!

MAKES 10–13 PIES

9 oz/250 g shortcrust pastry (pastry crust)
⅔ cup/200 g/7 oz mincemeat (see page 14)
a little milk
icing (confectioner's) sugar, sifted

Roll out the pastry on a floured surface to a thickness of ⅛ inch/3 mm. Cut out 10–13 circles using a 3 inch/7.5 cm cutter, and another 10–13 circles using a 2½ inch/6 cm cutter. Use the remaining scraps to cut out holly leaves or stars for decoration.

Place the larger circles in a tray of greased patty tins. Divide the mincemeat between the tins. Brush the edges of the smaller circles with a little cold water and place them on top of the pies. Press the edges together firmly. Snip a small hole in the centre of each pie, decorate with a holly leaf or star, and brush with a little milk.

Bake near the top of a preheated oven at 400°F/200°C/gas mark 6 for about 15 minutes until golden bown. Remove from the oven, sprinkle over a little sifted icing (confectioner's) sugar and allow to cool in the tins for 5 minutes before transferring to a wire rack. Store in an airtight tin. Serve either hot or cold with brandy butter.

BRANDY BUTTER

Nowadays, brandy butter is most commonly served with Christmas puddings and mince pies, though rum was the spirit originally used. This is an exceedingly good butter, whichever spirit you prefer. If you choose rum, use soft brown sugar and a few gratings of fresh nutmeg. It can be made well in advance, covered and refrigerated.

SERVES 8

½ cup/100 g/4 oz unsalted butter, softened
1 cup/100 g/4 oz icing (confectioner's) sugar, sifted
¼ cup/25 g/1 oz ground almonds
4 tbsp brandy
4 tbsp double (heavy) cream

Cream the butter until smooth and pale in colour. Gradually beat in the sugar and almonds. Finally add the brandy and cream. Fill into a serving bowl, cover and refrigerate.

*O*ur custom of lighting and decorating small fir trees for Christmas comes from Germany, where they symbolize loyalty and new life. Here the season begins at the start of Advent, when the first of four candles is lit in the Advent wreath – the others being lit on the remaining Sundays leading up to the Holy Evening.

On this evening, the family gathers before the trimmed tree and shares a meal. The next day, the Christkind, or Kriss Kringle, is credited with leaving behind sweets, fruits and gifts. Traditional German Christmas Day fare includes pork, game or goose, usually served with red cabbage and dumplings.

HALIBUT IN FENNEL AND SAFFRON

*I*n this recipe, a rich and creamy sauce complements the tender fish. But keep a close eye on the fish: halibut becomes very dry when it is overcooked.

SERVES 4

4 halibut fillets, each weighing about 5 oz/150 g
salt and freshly ground white pepper, flour to dust the fish
3 tbsp vegetable oil

FOR THE SAUCE:
2 tbsp/25 g/1 oz unsalted butter
1 shallot, finely chopped
½ small head of fennel, cut in half lengthwise, stalk removed and finely chopped
¼ cup/50 ml/2 fl oz white wine
½ cup plus 2 tbsp/150 ml/¼ pint fish stock
6 shreds of saffron
½ cup plus 2 tbsp/150 ml/¼ pint double (heavy) cream
1 tomato, peeled, deseeded and coarsely chopped
salt and freshly ground pepper, ½ tsp chopped dill

To make the sauce, heat the butter in a saucepan, add the shallots and fennel, and sweat until the shallots are translucent but not coloured. Add the wine and bring rapidly to the boil. Add the stock and saffron shreds. Return to the boil and simmer until the liquid is reduced to half its quantity. Add the cream and boil until creamy. Add the chopped tomato and return to the boil. Season, remove from the heat, and add the dill. Set aside.

Season the fish fillets. Dust with flour. Heat the vegetable oil in a non-stick pan, add the fish fillets and fry over medium heat for about 2 minutes, browning on both sides. Transfer to an ovenproof dish. Bake in a preheated oven at 325°F/170°C/gas mark 3 for about 8 minutes, depending on the thickness, or until cooked. Then remove from the oven and place on a warm serving dish. Reheat the sauce and pour over the fish.

ROAST GOOSE WITH ORANGE SAUCE

I prefer goose roasted simply in the oven and served with a piquant sauce. You'll be left with a lot of fat in your roasting tray – don't throw this away as it is delicious used for cooking braised cabbage or confit of onions, or simply spread on bread.

SERVES 6

10 lb/4.5 kg goose
salt and freshly ground white pepper
fresh rosemary and sage

FOR THE SAUCE:
the juice of 3 oranges
¼ cup/50 ml/2 fl oz orange liqueur such as Grand Marnier
1¼ cups/300 ml/½ pint chicken stock
1 pinch ground ginger
3 tsp cornflour (cornstarch)
salt and freshly ground pepper
1 large orange, peeled, divided into segments and cut into cubes

Season the goose with salt and pepper, then place the rosemary and sage in the cavity. Check the weight of the goose and calculate the cooking time, allowing 15 minutes per 1 lb/450 g, plus an additional 15 minutes. Put the goose on a wire rack in a roasting tray and place in the centre of a preheated oven at 425°F/220°C/gas mark 6. Roast for 20 minutes, then reduce the heat to 350°F/180°C/gas mark 4 and roast for about 2½ hours (or according to your calculated cooking time). Baste at regular intervals. To check that the goose is cooked, pierce the thickest part of the leg with a skewer – the juices must run clear with no trace of pink. Remove the goose from the roasting tray, place on a warm platter, and allow to rest for at least 20 minutes in a warm place before carving. Drain off the fat and reserve for future use.

To make the sauce, scrape off any burned bits from the roast-ing pan, and discard. Add the orange juice and liqueur. Add the chicken stock and ginger and bring to the boil. Allow to simmer for about 5 minutes. Mix the cornflour (cornstarch) with 2 tbsp of cold water in a small bowl, add a little of the boiling sauce to it, and mix well. Then whisk this mixture into the sauce in the roasting tray and bring back to the boil. Simmer until thickened. Season, pass the sauce through a fine sieve into a saucepan, and set aside.

Place the roasted goose on a serving dish. Bring the sauce to the boil, add the orange pieces and serve separately.

RIGHT: ROAST GOOSE WITH ORANGE SAUCE

MEDALLIONS OF PORK STUFFED WITH SAGE AND APRICOTS

These stuffed medallions of pork make a great alternative to roasting a whole goose. The tasty little parcels are wrapped in Parma ham and contain a fruity stuffing in the centre.

SERVES 4

8 medallions of pork, cut from a fillet, each about 2½ oz/65 g
4 slices Parma ham
2 tbsp vegetable oil

FOR THE STUFFING:
2 tbsp/25 g/1 oz butter
½ shallot, finely chopped
4 dried apricots, finely chopped
2 small leaves fresh sage, finely chopped
salt and freshly ground pepper

FOR THE SAUCE:
½ cup/100 ml/4 fl oz white wine
1 cup/250 ml/8 fl oz veal (or beef) stock
1 tbsp cornflour (cornstarch)
salt and freshly ground white pepper

Heat the butter in a small saucepan. Add the shallot and sweat until translucent but not coloured. Add the dried apricots and 2 tbsp of water. Cover with a lid and simmer very gently until the shallot and apricots are soft. Remove from the heat and season. Stir in the sage, then remove the mixture from the pan and spread on a flat plate to allow to cool quickly.

Carefully cut each of the medallions horizontally across to form a pocket, making sure that you do not cut it in half. Then divide the filling into 8 equal portions and fill the pocket of each medallion. Lightly press the pocket flat with your hand, and put to one side. Cut each slice of Parma ham in half lengthwise. Place the medallions on top of the ham slices and wrap each medallion to form a parcel.

Heat the vegetable oil in a frying pan. Season the medallions with pepper, and fry until golden brown on both sides. Transfer the medallions from the pan to a baking tray. Cook in a preheated oven at 350°F/180°C/gas mark 4 for 6–8 minutes, depending on the thickness of the meat.

To prepare the sauce, use the same frying pan. Add the wine. Bring to the boil. Simmer for 1 minute. Add the stock and return to the boil. In a small bowl mix the cornflour (cornstarch) with 2 tbsp water, then whisk this into the sauce in the pan. Return to the boil to thicken. Season, then pass through a fine sieve into a clean pan. Keep warm.

When the medallions are ready, place them on a serving dish and pour the sauce over.

BRAISED RED CABBAGE

The spoonful of pudding rice will disintegrate completely on cooking and will bind the liquid to give the cabbage a lovely shiny glaze.

SERVES 4

1 medium-sized red cabbage
2 tbsp vegetable oil
1 onion, sliced
1 apple, peeled, cored, cut lengthwise into 4 and thinly
sliced crosswise
¾ cup plus 2 tbsp/200 ml/7 fl oz red wine
1 tbsp pudding (shortgrain) rice
1 cup/250 ml/8 fl oz vegetable stock
salt and freshly ground white pepper
2 tbsp redcurrant jelly

Cut the cabbage into 4 pieces, removing the stalks with a knife. Cut each piece crosswise into fine strips, or slice with a shredder.

Heat the oil in a large saucepan. Add the onion and apple, and sweat until the onion is translucent but not coloured. Add the shredded cabbage and sweat again for a further 1 minute. Add the red wine, half the vegetable stock, and the rice. Stir, then cover and reduce the heat until the liquid is just simmering. Continue to simmer for about 1 hour, or until the cabbage is tender. Stir frequently while cooking, and top up with the remaining vegetable stock if necessary.

When the cabbage is cooked, remove the lid. There should be hardly any liquid left in the pan. Season, then add the redcurrant jelly, simmer for about 2 minutes and serve.

POTATO AND WALNUT GALETTES

These galettes make an unusual accompaniment to either the goose or pork dishes. The crunchy walnut coating encases creamy potato flavoured with nutmeg.

SERVES 4

1 lb/450 g old potatoes, peeled
2 tbsp/25 g/1 oz butter
2 eggs
1 tbsp chopped chives
salt and freshly ground pepper
nutmeg
1 cup/100 g/4 oz walnuts, finely chopped
flour for dusting the galettes
2–3 tbsp vegetable oil

Cut the potatoes into even-sized pieces. Place them in a pan of cold salted water and cover with a lid. Bring to the boil and simmer until cooked. Drain well, then place on a baking tray and dry inside a preheated oven at 325°F/170°C/gas mark 3 for about 5 minutes. Remove from the oven and rub through a fine sieve into a clean pan.

Place over medium heat and heat gently. Remove from the heat and immediately add the butter and seasoning. Lightly beat 1 of the eggs and add, whisking the mixture until smooth. Allow to cool (not in the refrigerator), then add the chives.

Divide the mixture into 8 equal portions. Shape each into a round shape 2¾ inches/7 cm in diameter and ¾ inch/2 cm thick. Lightly beat the other egg and place in a flat bowl. Place the walnuts on a plate. Place the flour on another plate. Dust each galette lightly in the flour, shaking off any excess, then coat each galette in egg, and then in the walnuts, ensuring that they are evenly covered. Set aside.

Heat the oil in a non-stick frying pan. Fry the galettes until evenly brown. Drain on kitchen towel for 1 minute, and serve.

BERRIES IN RUM WITH CINNAMON ICE-CREAM

During the summer in Germany, it is tradition to fill a Rumtopf pot with layers of assorted berries and then cover each layer with sugar and rum. When the pot is full, it is then left to mature. By Christmas Eve it is perfect to serve over ice-cream. This recipe has a similar effect. For the best results, use at least three different types of berry.

SERVES 4

½ cup plus 2 tbsp/150 ml/¼ pint rum
½ cup/100 ml/4 fl oz water
⅓ cup/75 g/3 oz caster (granulated) sugar
20 strawberries, cut in half and stalks removed
30 blueberries
20 raspberries
cinnamon ice-cream (page 31)

Place the rum, water and sugar in a saucepan large enough to hold the liquid and berries easily. Bring to the boil and add the strawberries and blueberries. Return to the boil and add the raspberries. Remove from the heat and mix gently with a wooden spoon. Cover with a lid and allow to cool. Leave to macerate overnight.

When you are ready to serve, pour the rum and berries into bowls, place 1 or 2 scoops of ice-cream in the centre of each bowl, and serve.

LEFT: BERRIES IN RUM WITH CINNAMON ICE-CREAM

*C*hristmas is a time of great festivity in Spain, with every home setting out the Nacimienlo, or Nativity Scene, lit with candles, while the streets are filled with sparkling lights and sounds of gaiety. On Christmas Eve, the church bells call to midnight Mass, after which there is more singing and dancing until the early hours when it is usual for the extended family to gather for the Christmas meal. I could not find a better person than Maria José Sevilla-Taylor, a good friend and passionate Spaniard from the Basque country, to tell me about the traditional Christmas feast, as it was prepared by her mother. The meal would be simple, starting with little dishes such as scampi, ham, prawn with garlic sauce, or a shellfish soup. As a main course, there was suckling pig or roasted lamb, and finally a compote of winter fruit.

SPANISH CHRISTMAS SOUP

*T*his full-flavoured fish broth, made with the freshest of ingredients, has a clean, irresistible flavour. Serve with slices of lightly toasted baguette.

SERVES 4

10 large fresh prawn (shrimps) in shells (no heads)
1 tbsp olive oil
1 shallot, sliced
⅛ tsp finely chopped chilli, seeds removed
½ clove garlic, sliced
12 medium-sized fresh mussels, cleaned
4 scampi (or large shrimp) tails in shells
¼ cup/50 ml/2 fl oz dry white wine
1¼ pints/800 ml/25 fl oz water
4 oz/100 g monkfish fillet, cubed into large pieces
2 slices dried ham, finely chopped
½ tsp finely chopped flat parsley
½ tsp finely chopped coriander (cilantro)
salt and freshly ground pepper
1 egg, hard-boiled and coarsely chopped

Peel the prawns (shrimps), reserving the shells, and cut the flesh into cubes. Heat the oil in a saucepan. Add the shells, mussels and scampi (shrimp) tails, then the shallot, chilli and garlic. Sweat until the shallots are transparent but not coloured. Add the white wine and water, and bring to the boil. Simmer gently for 15 minutes. Pass the liquid through a fine muslin cloth into another pan, and set aside. Remove the mussels from the shells. Remove the shells carefully from the scampi (shrimp) tails, and cut the flesh into half lengthwise. Discard the shells.

Bring the stock to the boil, then reduce the heat. Add the mussels and the prawn (shrimp) and monkfish cubes. Remove from the heat and add the ham, parsley, coriander (cilantro) and scampi (shrimp) tails. Season, add the chopped egg and serve.

ABOVE: SPANISH CHRISTMAS SOUP

BRAISED SHOULDER OF LAMB

This recipe is simplicity itself. The flavours of the garlic and fresh rosemary combine to produce a dish that smells heavenly, tastes delicious and melts in the mouth.

SERVES 4

2 tbsp olive oil
4 cloves garlic, whole
1 sprig rosemary
1 medium-sized shoulder of lamb
salt and freshly ground pepper
2 medium potatoes, peeled and cut into 1½ inch/4 cm cubes
½ cup/100 ml/4 fl oz dry white wine
1¼ cups/300 ml/½ pint lamb (or beef) stock

Heat the oil in a non-stick pan. Add the garlic and rosemary, and brown over medium heat until golden. Remove from the heat.

Season the lamb, place in a casserole dish, and spoon the garlic and rosemary mixture on top. Then add the potato cubes, the wine and three-quarters of the stock. Bring to the boil, cover and cook in a preheated oven at 350°F/180°C/gas mark 4 for about 1 hour or until the potatoes are cooked. Then remove the potatoes and keep warm. Add the remaining stock to the casserole and return to the oven for another 30 minutes. When cooked, the meat should be golden brown and tender, with a little sauce left in the bottom of the casserole dish.

Serve straight from the dish, or remove the lamb and place on a serving dish with the potatoes.

LEFT: BRAISED SHOULDER OF LAMB

SIMPLY ROASTED POUSSIN FLAVOURED WITH LEMON GRASS AND ROSEMARY

An alternative to the lamb that's just as easy. The unusual combination of ingredients used here make this dish a real winner. Serve with roast potatoes (see page 54).

SERVES 4

4 poussins (young chickens), each weighing about 1 lb/450 g
2 cloves garlic, cut in half lengthwise
2 sticks lemon grass, cut in half
zest of 1 clementine (clementine orange)
2 sprigs of fresh rosemary
salt and freshly ground pepper
4 tbsp vegetable oil

TO GARNISH:
3 tbsp/40 g/1½ oz butter
¼ tsp finely chopped clementine (clementine orange) zest
4 small sprigs of rosemary

First prepare the poussins by placing half a clove of garlic, half a stick of lemon grass, a piece of clementine skin and a sprig of rosemary inside each bird. Season the skin with salt and freshly ground pepper.

Heat a shallow roasting tray in a preheated oven at 400°F/200°C/gas mark 6, then add the vegetable oil. Place the poussins on the tray, breast side uppermost. Roast for 30 minutes or until cooked and golden brown, basting frequently. Remove from the oven and allow to rest for at least 5 minutes before placing on a serving dish.

In a small pan, brown the butter until foaming, add the rosemary and chopped clementine skin, and pour this over the poussins.

BAKED PEPPERS WITH BLACK OLIVES

Baking the peppers gives them a really intense flavour, which complements the simplicity of either the lamb or the poussins perfectly. For the best effect use a variety of different-coloured peppers.

SERVES 4

2 tbsp olive oil
4 medium-sized sweet (bell) peppers (green, yellow or red)
2 cloves garlic, peeled and cut in half lengthwise
1 small sprig thyme
12 black olives, pitted
salt and freshly ground pepper

Cut the peppers in half lengthwise, remove the stems and pips with a small knife, and cut roughly into 1 inch/2½ cm cubes.

Heat a shallow roasting tray and add the olive oil. Add the peppers, garlic and sprig of thyme and bake in a preheated oven at 375°F/190°C/gas mark 5 for 10–12 minutes until cooked and slightly browned. Season with salt and freshly ground pepper. Add the olives, leaving them for 1 minute to heat through. Transfer from the tray into a serving dish with a slotted spoon, and serve.

DRIED FRUIT COMPOTE

This compote of dried fruits and chestnuts is a very Christmassy dish, which can be prepared well in advance. Serve at room temperature with a scoop of walnut ice-cream (see page 31).

SERVES 4

⅓ cup/50 g/2 oz dried figs
½ cup/100 g/4 oz dried prunes
⅔ cup/100 g/4 oz dried apricots
⅓ cup/50 g/2 oz sultanas (sultana raisins)
⅔ cup/100 g/4 oz dried apple
½ cup/100 g/4 oz caster (granulated) sugar
½ cup/100 g/4 oz chestnuts, peeled
1 tbsp sherry
2 tbsp white wine
1 pear, peeled, cored and sliced

FOR THE SYRUP:
¼ cup/50 g/2 oz caster (granulated) sugar
½ cup plus 2 tbsp/150 ml/¼ pint water
juice of 1 orange
½ cinnamon stick
1 vanilla pod

TO GARNISH:
walnut ice-cream (page 31)
15 walnuts, coarsely chopped
fresh mint leaves
icing (confectioner's) sugar to dust the finished dish

Soak all the dried fruits overnight in water. Drain, rinse and keep aside.

Place the sugar in a saucepan over medium heat. Do not stir. Allow the sugar to turn golden brown, then remove from the heat and set aside to cool. Add the sherry and white wine, and bring to the boil. Simmer for a few minutes until the caramelized sugar is dissolved. Stir and add the chestnuts. Add enough water to just cover the chestnuts, cover with a lid and simmer for 15 minutes or until the chestnuts are cooked. Remove the pan from the heat and allow to cool. Set aside.

To prepare the syrup, put all the ingredients into a saucepan large enough to hold all the dried fruits and chestnuts. Place over gentle heat and allow the sugar to dissolve. Bring to the boil, then add all the dried fruits and return to the boil. Add the sliced pear and chestnuts with their liquid. Stir gently and cook for a further 2–3 minutes. Remove from the heat and allow to cool in the pan. Remove the vanilla pod and cinnamon stick.

Spoon the compote on to plates, add a scoop of ice-cream, sprinkle with walnuts, garnish with mint leaves and dust with icing (confectioner's) sugar.

*E*very Christmas brings back memories of my childhood – a comparatively humble affair, spent quietly with family. It was the one day of the year when my grandfather closed the hotel in the evening so that – like other Swiss families – we were able to gather together. This would take place in front of our enormous tree, which had always been beautifully decorated the day before with my grandmother's collection of antique baubles and real candles, which were lit on Christmas Eve when the hotel closed. Here we would sing carols, exchange gifts and, at midnight, listen to the famous bells of Zurich calling the faithful to Mass. Our meal always included a ham either wrapped in bread dough or glazed with honey and spiked with cloves, simply served with a delicious potato salad.

SMOKED TROUT AND HORSERADISH PARFAIT

*T*his recipe is easy to make and can be prepared well in advance. The creamy parfait is delicious served with warm slices of toasted baguette.

SERVES 4

12 oz/350 g smoked salmon, thinly sliced
12 oz/350 g smoked trout fillet, with no skin or bones
½ cup plus 2 tbsp/150 g/5 oz butter, at room temperature
½ cup/100 g/4 oz cream cheese
½ tsp creamed horseradish
salt and freshly ground white pepper
1 tsp chopped dill

TO GARNISH:
1 cucumber, salmon roe, caviar, chervil, dill

Line 4 ramekin dishes with the smoked salmon. Ensure that the slices hang over the edges of the ramekins. Put to one side.

Process the smoked trout, butter and cream cheese in a blender or food processor until smooth. Add the creamed horseradish. Taste and season. Fold the dill into the mixture. Divide between the 4 ramekin dishes, and smooth the surface evenly. Fold over the overlapping edges of the smoked salmon. Keep in the refrigerator overnight.

About 30–40 minutes before serving, turn the salmon parcels out on to a tray, and leave at room temperature to allow the filling to soften.

Cut the cucumber into thin slices and place them in a circle (slightly larger than the ramekin) in the centre of each plate. Gently lift the salmon parcels on to the centre of the plates. Garnish the top with salmon roe and caviar, and finish with chervil and dill.

ABOVE: HONEY-GLAZED HAM WITH CLOVES

HONEY-GLAZED HAM WITH CLOVES

The number of cloves you will need depends on personal preference. I like an intense flavour so use about 10. Obviously you can use less. Accompany with warm bread sauce (see page 54).

SERVES 4–6

3.3 lb/1.5 kg cured ham, rolled (no bone)
1 onion, peeled
½ bay leaf
3 tbsp honey
½ tsp English (Colman's) mustard
5–10 cloves
2 tbsp icing (confectioner's) sugar

Soak the ham in cold water for at least 1 hour, or preferably overnight. Discard the soaking water and place the ham in a large saucepan. Cover completely with cold water. Bring to the boil, removing any impurities with a ladle. Add the onion and bay leaf. Cover the saucepan with a lid, then reduce the heat and simmer very gently for about 1 hour 40 minutes until cooked.

Remove the ham and place on an oven tray. Reserve the cooking liquid, which makes a wonderful stock for soup. In a small saucepan, dissolve the mustard in a tablespoon of cold water and mix together with the honey. Heat gently, then remove from the heat and set aside.

Remove any skin and string from the ham and turn gently until the best side of the ham is uppermost. Spike this side with cloves, and brush with the mustard and honey mixture. Give the ham a good dusting of sugar and bake in a preheated oven at 400°F/200°C/gas mark 6 for 30 minutes until a golden-brown crust forms. Remove from the oven, and serve.

RIGHT: MERINGUE WITH CHESTNUT PURÉE

POTATO AND PEAR SALAD

This rustic salad is reminiscent of the one my mother used to make. The addition of a pear adds a subtle sweetness which complements the ham perfectly.

SERVES 4

1 ripe pear
1 lb/450 g small to medium potatoes
salad leaves, sliced tomato or hard-boiled egg to garnish

FOR THE DRESSING:
1 tbsp mild mustard
1 tbsp vegetable oil
½ small onion, finely chopped
½ clove garlic, crushed
½ cup plus 2 tbsp/150 ml/5 fl oz vegetable stock
¼ cup/50 ml/2 fl oz white wine vinegar
salt and freshly ground pepper
2 tsp chopped chives

Peel the pear, cut it into quarters, then remove the core and pips. Cook in boiling water for about 8 minutes and allow to cool. Remove from the cooking liquid with a perforated spoon and dry on kitchen paper. Cut into thin slices, and place in a large bowl. Cook the potatoes in their skins and peel while still warm. Cut into thin slices; mix gently together with the pears.

To make the dressing, heat the oil in a non-stick pan, add the onions and crushed garlic, and sweat until the onions are translucent but not coloured. Add the stock. Boil for 2 minutes, then remove from the heat. Whisk the vinegar and mustard in, and season. Pour the hot dressing immediately over the pears and potatoes.

Allow the salad to rest for about 30 minutes, then gently mix in the chopped chives. Arrange in a serving bowl and garnish.

LEMON BEAN SALAD

Any variation of dried beans can be used in this salad to make a tasty alternative. An easy way to mix the dressing is to place all the ingredients in a jar, seal securely with the lid and shake well.

SERVES 4

⅔ cup/100 g/4 oz dried haricot beans, soaked overnight in cold water
8 oz/225 g fine French beans, topped and tailed
4 spring onions, dark green leaves removed
1 egg, hard-boiled and peeled
2 medium tomatoes
1 tbsp finely chopped flat-leaf parsley, to garnish

FOR THE DRESSING:
6 tbsp olive oil
grated rind and juice of 1 small lemon
1 clove garlic, crushed
salt and freshly ground black pepper

Drain the haricot beans and place in fresh unsalted water. Bring to the boil and simmer for about 45 minutes until tender. While the haricot beans are cooking, mix the dressing ingredients together. Set aside. Drain the haricot beans, rinse in cold water, and place in a bowl.

Cut the French beans in half. Bring a pot of salted water to the boil, add the beans, return to the boil and simmer for 2–3 minutes, until cooked but still slightly crunchy. Drain, refresh under cold water, and add to the haricot beans.

Chop the spring onions into fine circles. Add to the beans. Pour over the dressing and toss gently. Pile into a salad bowl. Chop the egg finely and sprinkle on top. Finally, slice the tomatoes into wedges or slices, and arrange around the edge of the dish. Sprinkle with chopped parsley and serve.

MERINGUE WITH CHESTNUT PURÉE

This chestnut dessert takes me right back to my childhood! This version is sophisticated, rich and delicious. Especially when served with vanilla ice-cream and hot chocolate sauce.

SERVES 8

4 egg whites
1 cup plus 2 tbsp/225 g/8 oz caster (granulated) sugar
1 tsp arrowroot

FOR THE FILLING:
4 whole candied chestnuts (optional)
½ cup plus 2 tbsp/150 ml/5 fl oz double (heavy) cream
1 tbsp milk
1 x 9 oz/250 g can sweetened chestnut purée

Start by lining 2 baking trays with silicone paper. Draw a circle about 7 inches/17.5 cm in diameter on each of the trays. To make the meringue, ensure that your bowl and whisk are clean and dry. Then whisk the egg whites until very stiff. Add 1 tbsp of the sugar and continue to whisk until the mixture holds a peak. Add the remaining sugar and arrowroot and fold in. Using half the mixture, spread it on to one of the circles. Use the remaining mixture to form the other circle. Alternatively, use a piping bag with a plain ½ inch/1 cm nozzle and pipe the mixture on each tray.

Bake in a preheated oven at 275°F/140°C/gas mark 1 until quite dry. Remove from the silicone paper and allow to cool on a wire rack.

To make the filling, chop the whole candied chestnuts and put to one side. Gently whip half the cream and milk until it forms soft peaks. Then fold in the chestnut purée and the chopped candied chestnuts.

Spread the filling evenly over 1 of the meringue circles. Place the other circle on top. Before serving, whip the remaining cream and pipe a circle of rosettes around the edge.

$\mathscr{S}$cotland is definitely the place to be on New Year's Eve, or Hogmanay, when – after a somewhat subdued Christmas – the Scots really come into their own. Traditionally, every home should be cleaned and tidied before the New Year, and then the biggest fire that the fireplace can hold is lit to burn out the old year while family and friends gather to celebrate. While researching for this book, I was told by a Scotsman that his family always served steak pie for this celebration. I've learned since that the pie often includes a few sausages, too. After eating, the revelry goes on through the night and often centres on huge bonfires lit outdoors. At the stroke of midnight, great slices of 'Black Bun' are washed down by many 'het pints' of spiced ale mixed with eggs and whisky.

SHRIMPS AND SALMON WITH SOURED CREAM

This is so simple, but a real winner. If you don't have metal rings, serve potted in 2 inch/5 cm ramekin dishes. Warm Melba toast would accompany this well.

SERVES 4

5 oz/150 g small cooked shrimps, roughly chopped
5 oz/150 g smoked salmon, finely diced
2 oz/50 g shallots, finely chopped
1 tsp finely chopped chives
2 tsp mild white wine vinegar
4 tsp sunflower oil
1 tsp creamed horseradish
salt and freshly ground white pepper
¾ cup/150 ml/6 fl oz crème fraîche (or sour cream)

TO GARNISH:
1 cucumber, cut into ⅛ inch/3 mm cubes, 4 sprigs dill or chervil, salmon roe

Gently mix together the shrimps, smoked salmon, shallots and chives. Whisk together the vinegar, oil and creamed horseradish, and add this to the shrimp and salmon mixture. Season to taste and set aside.

Place 4 metal rings about 2¾ inches/7 cm in diameter on to a small flat tray. Spoon the mixture in equal amounts into the rings and press down lightly. Spread the crème fraîche (or sour cream) in equal amounts on top of each ring and smooth over the surface. Refrigerate for at least 30 minutes.

Arrange the cucumber slices in the centre of the plates to form a circle. Remove the metal rings gently from the shrimp and salmon mixture, then carefully lift these off with a palette knife and place in the centre of the cucumber. Spoon a little roe on top and garnish with dill or chervil.

ABOVE: SHRIMPS AND SALMON WITH SOURED CREAM

SPICY STEAK PIE WITH A WALNUT CRUST

An extra-special pie that looks and tastes exceptional. Make it in advance and pop it into the oven when required. The pastry is quick and easy to make, but if you're short of time you could use some ready-made puff pastry instead. Marinating the meat tenderizes it and adds to the flavour, which is rich, spicy and deliciously festive.

SERVES 4

1⅓ cup/225 g/8 oz plain flour
½ tsp salt
¾ cup/175 g/6 oz butter, frozen
½ cup/100 ml/4 fl oz ice-cold water
⅔ cup/75 g/3 oz walnuts, finely chopped
1 egg yolk, beaten, to glaze

FOR THE FILLING:
2 lb/900 g lean stewing steak
½ cup plus 2 tbsp/150 ml/¼ pint red wine
2 large cloves garlic, crushed

1 tsp whole juniper berries, crushed
6 cloves
¼ whole nutmeg, grated
4 tbsp oil
6 tbsp/75 g/3 oz butter
1 cup/50 g/2 oz button onions, peeled
2 cups/100 g/4 oz button mushrooms, trimmed
4 medium carrots, peeled
½ cup/50 g/2 oz plain flour
½ tsp salt
freshly ground black pepper
1¼ cups/300 ml/½ pint beef stock

To make the pastry, sift the flour and salt into a bowl. Grate the frozen butter directly into it. Then cut the butter into the flour until the mixture is crumbly. Sprinkle over the walnuts. Now gradually add the ice-cold water, mixing with the knife until you can gather the dough into a ball with your hands. Place in a plastic bag and refrigerate for 1 hour or overnight.

To make the filling, trim the meat and cut into large cubes. Place in a flat dish and pour over the red wine. Add the crushed garlic, juniper berries, cloves and nutmeg. Mix, ensuring that the meat is well soaked. Cover with clingfilm and refrigerate for at least 4 hours, or preferably overnight.

The following day, prepare the vegetables: leave the onions and mushrooms whole, but cut the carrots into 4 lengthwise and then into 1 inch/2.5 cm pieces. Heat 2 tbsp oil and half the butter in a large frying pan. Add the vegetables and toss over medium heat until the onions start to colour. Transfer with a slotted spoon to a deep pot.

Now remove the meat from the marinade with the slotted spoon, and pat dry with kitchen towel. Put the flour, salt and pepper into a large plastic bag, add the meat and toss. Add the remaining oil and butter to the frying pan. When it is hot, add the beef in batches and brown thoroughly on all sides, transferring it to the vegetables in the deep pot as it is ready.

Finally, remove the 6 cloves from the marinade and pour it into the frying pan. Stir, add the stock, and boil to thicken, then add to the meat and vegetables. Cover and simmer gently for 1½–2 hours, or until the meat is tender. Check regularly to ensure that it is not catching at the bottom of the pan. Remove from the heat and pour into a 2½ pint/1¾ litre pie dish. Place a pie funnel in the centre and cool.

Roll out the pastry to a thickness of about ¼ inch/5 mm. Cut a strip about ½ inch/1 cm wide and long enough to run all around the top lip of the pie dish. Moisten with a little water and press gently on to the dish. Now cut out the pie lid. Moisten the edge with a little water and place on top of the pie. Press gently to seal to the pastry lip. Make a small hole in the centre with a sharp knife. Use the trimmings to cut out the letters to read 'Happy New Year', or the date of the new year. Brush with the beaten egg yolk, then bake in the centre of the preheated oven at 325°F/170°C/gas mark 3 for 35 minutes until golden brown.

SWEDE (RUTABAGA) AND POTATO PURÉE WITH CHIVES

Mashed swede (rutabaga), or 'bashed neeps', is popularly served in Scotland through the winter months. Mixing it with potato makes it more subtle in flavour and ideal to serve with a hearty dish.

SERVES 4

5 medium-sized potatoes, peeled and cut into thumb-sized pieces
2 tbsp vegetable oil
½ medium swede (rutabaga), peeled and cut into 1 inch/2.5 cm cubes
1 small onion, finely chopped
½ cup plus 2 tbsp/150 ml/¼ pint vegetable stock
¼ cup/50 ml/2 fl oz single (light) cream
2 tbsp/25 g/1 oz butter, cut into small cubes
salt and freshly ground pepper
2 tbsp finely chopped chives

Cook the potatoes until tender.

Heat the vegetable oil in a saucepan, add the swede (rutabaga) cubes and chopped onion, and sweat over medium heat until the onions are translucent but not coloured. Add the vegetable stock and bring to the boil. Then reduce the heat, cover with a lid and simmer until the swede (rutabaga) is completely cooked. Remove the saucepan from the heat and remove the pieces. Squeeze them gently with the back of a spoon and pour any excess liquid back into the pan. Return the liquid to the heat and simmer until there is just about 1 tbsp left. Remove from the heat.

Now place the potatoes and swede (rutabaga) into a saucepan large enough to hold them both easily. Add the cream and the cooking liquid, and bring to the boil. Add the butter. Keeping the saucepan over low heat, use a masher to mash the potatoes and swede (rutabaga) to a purée. Remove from the heat and season with salt and pepper. Finally, add the chopped chives and serve.

RIGHT: SPICY STEAK PIE WITH A WALNUT CRUST

BLACK BUN WITH HOGMANAY CREAM

A bun is an old Scottish word for a plum cake. This one, traditionally served at Hogmanay, is very dark, concentrated with a mass of fruits and succulent with whisky. The cake is encased in pastry to keep in the juices while cooking. Needless to say, the bun is delicious and matures beautifully. Make it at least two weeks before using. At the Hogmanay gathering, black bun is traditionally washed down with copious quantities of 'het pints' – spiced ale mixed with eggs and whisky. I prefer to serve mine in thick slices with iced Hogmanay cream.

SERVES 8

1¾ cups/175 g/6 oz plain flour
1 tsp ground cinnamon
1 tsp ground ginger
2 tsp ground allspice
1 tsp ground nutmeg
½ tsp black pepper
½ tsp baking powder
½ tsp cream of tartar
½ cup/100 g/4 oz dark brown sugar
3 cups/450 g/1 lb seedless raisins
3 cups/450 g/1 lb currants
½ cup/50 g/2 oz candied peel
1 cup/100 g/4 oz blanched almonds, flaked or chopped
3 tbsp milk
8 tbsp whisky
1 egg, lightly beaten
17 oz/500 g shortcrust pastry (pastry crust)
1 egg yolk, lightly beaten
caster (granulated) sugar to serve

FOR THE HOGMANAY CREAM:
2⅔ cups/1 litre/1¾ pints vanilla ice-cream (page 31)
5 tbsp/75 ml/3 fl oz whisky

To make the filling, sift together the flour, spices, pepper, baking powder and cream of tartar. Add the sugar, dried fruits, peel and nuts. Pour over the milk, whisky and beaten egg. Mix together well.

On a floured board, using two-thirds of the pastry, roll it out thinly. Line the base and sides of a greased round 9 inch/23 cm x 2 in/5 cm spring-form tin, ensuring that the pastry overhangs the top of the sides of the tin. Spoon in the filling, ensuring that it is level, and press down firmly.

Roll out the remaining pastry to a 9 inch/23 cm circle. Moisten the edges with a little water and place it on top of the filling. Press the edges together firmly, trim the excess off and crimp decoratively. Leftover bits can be used to decorate ('Happy New Year' or the date of the year, etc.).

Lastly, using a long skewer, make 4 holes all the way through to the base. Brush lightly with the beaten egg yolk and bake in the centre of a preheated oven at 325°F/170°C/gas mark 3 for 2½–3 hours. After 1 hour, check the cake. If the pastry is browning too rapidly, cover with foil. The bun is cooked when a thin skewer, inserted through the middle, comes out clean.

Allow to cool slightly before turning out. Cool on a wire rack and store in an airtight tin or wrapped in foil for at least 2 weeks.

Just before serving, make the hogmanay cream. Place the ice-cream in a liquidizer or food processor. Add the whisky and blend for about 30 seconds until well combined. Pour into 4 tall glasses, add a straw and serve with a thick slice of black bun, sprinkled with sugar.

*N*ew Year's Eve is probably the busiest night for celebrations the world over. For me and my team, this means a long night – not of partying but of preparing hundreds of meals for our guests! Normally, we serve a lavish five-course meal, where food and wine are matched in perfect harmony. When the clock strikes midnight and the piper walks through the rooms, hundreds of champagne corks pop as friends drink a toast to the New Year. Back home in Switzerland, it was traditional for the chef to walk through the room, not with bagpipes but with a live suckling pig in his arms! Everyone who touched it was assured luck for the next 365 days of the year. My work usually ends at about 2 a.m., when I fall exhausted into bed. New Year celebrations are reserved for later in the day…

'And God send you a Happy New Year.'

SMOKED HADDOCK AND ASPARAGUS TARTLETS

*T*his recipe makes four small tartlets. If preferred, make one large tart, but increase the cooking time, and serve in slices. Be sure that you taste the filling before seasoning and only add salt if necessary.

SERVES 4

5 oz/150 g shortcrust pastry (pastry crust)
flour to dust the dough
1 egg, lightly beaten

FOR THE FILLING:
12 pieces medium-sized asparagus, cooked in salted water,
refreshed and cut into small pieces
½ shallot, finely chopped
5 oz/150 g fresh smoked haddock fillet, coarsely chopped
½ tsp finely chopped chives
½ cup plus 2 tbsp/150 ml/¼ pint double (heavy) cream
1 egg, lightly beaten
salt and freshly ground pepper

FOR THE DRESSING:
2 tbsp white wine vinegar
1 pinch English (Colman's) mustard
1 tsp lime juice
¼ tbsp honey
5 tbsp sunflower oil
salt and freshly ground pepper

FOR THE SALAD:
a selection of salad leaves such as radicchio, corn salad, curly
endive, rocket and oak leaves

TO GARNISH:
12 pieces fine asparagus, cooked, refreshed and cut in half
sprigs of fresh chervil and dill

Start by greasing 4 flan tins or loose-bottomed tartlet moulds about 4 inches/10 cm in diameter and ½ inch/1 cm deep. Lightly dust the pastry dough with flour and roll it out to a thickness of about ⅛ inch/3 mm. Then, using a round cutter or knife, cut out 4 discs at least ½ inch/1 cm larger than the flan tins. Press the discs lightly into the greased flan tins, then line with greaseproof paper and fill with dried beans. Bake blind in the lower part of the preheated oven at 375°F/190°C/gas mark 5 for about 10 minutes.

Take the pastry cases out of the oven and remove the paper and beans. Brush each case with a little of the beaten egg and return to the oven for another 5 minutes, to seal the pastry and prevent the cases becoming soggy when the filling is added to them. Remove the tartlet cases from the oven and put to one side.

To make the filling, mix together the asparagus, shallot, smoked haddock and chives in a bowl. Add the cream and egg, and season with salt and pepper if necessary.

Divide the asparagus and smoked haddock mixture equally between the 4 tartlet cases, and bake in the oven for 18–20 minutes, or until the filling is set and golden brown.

While the tartlets are baking, make the dressing. To do this, simply mix together all the ingredients and set aside.

When the tartlets are cooked, remove them from the oven and allow to rest for 5 minutes. Meanwhile, toss the salad leaves in the dressing and arrange on 4 plates. Then carefully remove each tartlet from its flan tin, and place in the centre of the salad. To add a final touch, garnish with fine asparagus, and scatter with chervil and dill.

RIGHT: SMOKED HADDOCK AND ASPARAGUS TARTLETS

PAN-FRIED FILLET STEAK WITH BLUE CHEESE SAUCE

This steak is served with a really gutsy sauce. The basis can be prepared in advance, but reserve the mustard, cheese and herbs to be added just before serving.

SERVES 4

1 tbsp vegetable oil
4 fillet steaks
salt and freshly ground white pepper

FOR THE SAUCE:
1 tbsp vegetable oil
1 shallot, finely chopped
2 cups/100 g/4 oz button mushrooms, sliced
¼ cup/50 ml/2 fl oz white wine
½ cup/100 ml/4 fl oz beef stock
1 cup/250 ml/8 fl oz single (light) cream
1 tbsp grain mustard
1 tbsp blue cheese, finely cubed
salt and freshly ground white pepper
2 tsp finely chopped parsley
1 tbsp finely chopped chives

Heat the oil in a non-stick pan. Season the steak and brown on both sides. Reduce the heat and cook to your required degree (for medium, about 7–10 minutes; for rare just under 5 minutes). Remove the pan from the heat and keep the steak warm in a serving dish.

To make the sauce, using the same pan, heat the oil. Add the shallot and sweat until translucent but not coloured. Add the mushrooms and sweat for a further minute. Add the wine and stock, and bring to the boil. Simmer gently to reduce to half its quantity. Add the cream and simmer until you obtain a creamy consistency. Remove from the heat and whisk in the mustard. Add the blue cheese, parsley and chives. Season to taste. Pour the sauce over the steak and serve hot.

LEFT: PAN-FRIED FILLET STEAK WITH BLUE CHEESE SAUCE

POTATO AND SHALLOT BAKE

A full-flavoured potato dish that is ideal with steak. It's also good served with a roast joint of meat or in the summer with a barbecue.

SERVES 4

1 tsp vegetable oil
3 shallots, peeled and finely sliced
salt and freshly ground pepper
1½ lb/675 g potatoes, peeled and finely sliced
2¼ cups/500 ml/16 fl oz chicken or vegetable stock
2 tbsp grated Parmesan cheese
2 tbsp/25 g/1 oz butter

Heat the vegetable oil in a non-stick pan. Add the shallots, season with salt and pepper, and sweat, covered, over low to medium heat for about 8 minutes. Stir regularly until the shallots are slightly browned. Remove from the heat and set aside.

Butter an ovenproof dish and arrange the potatoes in it in layers alternately with the shallots, finishing with a layer of potato slices overlapping each other. Pour the stock over and gently press the potatoes down, making sure that they are completely covered with stock.

Bake in a preheated oven at 325°F/170°C/gas mark 3 for about 1 hour. Then remove from the oven, dot with the remaining butter, sprinkle with Parmesan and bake for 10 minutes. Remove from the oven, cover with foil and bake for a further 20 minutes until the potatoes are cooked and golden brown.

SAUTÉED GREEN BEANS AND MUSHROOMS

This is a simple and tasty dish. Cook the beans in advance and just finish off before serving. It is advisable to toss the beans and mushrooms in small amounts rather than all at once.

SERVES 4

1 lb/450 g thin French beans, topped and tailed
1 tbsp olive oil
2 tbsp/25 g/1 oz unsalted butter
1 shallot, finely chopped
8 button mushrooms, thinly sliced
salt and freshly ground white pepper

Cook the French beans in boiling salted water until tender but still crisp. Refresh and drain, then set aside.

Heat the olive oil in a large non-stick pan. Add the butter and mushrooms, and toss quickly. Add the shallot and sweat for about 1 minute. Add the cooked beans, mix thoroughly with the mushrooms, season and heat through. Place in a serving dish and serve.

CHOCOLATE FEAST

Being a committed chocoholic, I think this has got to be my all-time favourite dessert. The combination of flavours and textures is wonderful and totally extravagant! Make up the cake, mousse, ice-cream and chocolate sauce in advance. Assemble just before serving.

SERVES 6

scant 1 cup/125 g/4½ oz plain flour
1½ tbsp cocoa, sifted
½ tsp bicarbonate of soda (baking soda)
⅓ cup/125 g/4½ oz sugar
¼ tsp salt
2½ tbsp oil
½ tbsp vinegar
½ tsp vanilla
¼ cup/125 ml/4½ fl oz water

FOR THE CHOCOLATE SAUCE:
7 oz/200 g plain chocolate, chopped finely
1 x 6 oz/170 g can evaporated milk
½ cup/100 ml/4 fl oz single (light) cream

FOR THE MOUSSE:
4½ oz/125 g plain chocolate, chopped finely
2 tbsp/25 g/1 oz butter
2 small eggs, separated
1 tbsp/15 g/½ oz caster (granulated) sugar
½ cup plus 1 tbsp/125 ml/4½ fl oz double (heavy) cream

TO SERVE:
2½ cups/600 ml/1 pint caramel crunch ice-cream (page 31)
½ cup plus 2 tbsp/150 ml/5 fl oz double (heavy)
cream, whipped

Mix together the flour, cocoa, bicarbonate of soda (baking soda), sugar and salt. Make a well in the centre and pour in the oil, vinegar and water. Stir vigorously with a wooden spoon until blended. Alternatively, blend all the ingredients together in a food processor. Pour into a lined and greased 1 lb/450 g loaf tin. Bake in a preheated oven at 350°F/180°C/gas mark 4 for about 20 minutes until cooked. Cool, then turn out.

To make the chocolate sauce, heat the milk and cream together in a saucepan until boiling. Turn the heat to low. Add the chopped chocolate and whisk until it has melted and the sauce is smooth. Do not boil. Remove from the heat and use, hot or cold, as required.

To make the mousse, melt together the chocolate and butter. My preferred method for doing this is to pop them into an ovenproof bowl and into a warm oven at 180°F/90°C/gas mark ¾ until just melted. Allow to cool slightly.

Whisk together the egg yolks and sugar until pale and mousse-like. Continue whisking, and add the chocolate spoon by spoon.

Wash your whisk and ensure that it is completely clean and dry. Now beat the egg whites until stiff. In another bowl, whip the cream until thick. Now add the cream and egg whites to the chocolate mixture and fold together gently. Pour into a bowl, cover and allow to set in the refrigerator overnight.

Before you sit down to eat, get everything ready, so that assembling the dessert at the last minute is simple. Using a sharp knife, remove the crust from the cake, then slice six ½ inch/1 cm slices from the cake and put to one side. Whip the cream until thick and spoon into a piping bag fitted with a star nozzle. Keep refrigerated. Pour the chocolate sauce into a pan to warm gently when required. Remove the ice-cream from the freezer and allow it 40 minutes in the refrigerator to soften.

To assemble the dessert, place a slice of cake on each plate. Top each slice with a scoop of chocolate mousse and another of ice-cream. Decorate with the whipped cream and finally drizzle over the warm chocolate sauce. Serve immediately.

INDEX

ACKNOWLEDGEMENTS

Courtesy of the Bridgeman Art Library: page 1 Fra Angelico, *Adoration of the Kings,* National Gallery, London; 8 Frederick Daniel Hardy, *Christmas Visitors Stirring the Pudding,* Christie's, London; 16 Taborda Viame Carlos, *Four Angels Playing Instruments,* National Museum of Ancient Art, Lisbon, Giraudon/Bridgeman; 25 Kate Greenaway, 'Supper', from *Christmas in Little Peopleton Manor* in *Illustrated London News,* Christmas 1879, Victoria and Albert Museum, London; 33 Melozzo da Forli, *Angel Musician,* Vatican Museums & Galleries, Rome; 37 Viggo Johansen, *Happy Christmas,* Hirschsprungske Samling, Copenhagen; 42 Father Christmas with punch, Collection Kharbine, Paris; 48 English School, *Winter Scene,* Philip Gale Fine Art, Chepstow; 57 Christmas Tree festooned, Victoria & Albert Museum, London; Anonymous, central panel of an altarpiece dedicated to St Vincent the Martyr of Saragossa, Museo Diocesano de Lerida, Catalunya, Index/Bridgeman; 70 Rudolph, *Gathering for Christmas Dinner,* private collection; 75 Francesco Botticini, *Angel Playing the Bagpipe,* Museo Della Collgiata di Sant' Andrea, Empoli; 81 Andrea Mategna, *Adoration of the Magi,* J. Paul Getty Museum, California.